"THE WILDERNESS THAT BECAME LAWRENCE"

by
The Eighth Grade Class
Lawrence Elementary School

Limited Edition
Lawrence Elementary School
Rt. #5
Marietta, Ohio 45750
Copyright©1976

TABLE OF CONTENTS

FOREWORD

This project began in the Fall of 1974. At that time my 7th grade class began asking some local history questions for which I had no answers. I promised to look into the matter. After researching several libraries, I found no works done exclusively about Lawrence Township. We decided to do our own research on the subject.

The first months consisted of collecting information already written about Lawrence Township. As each bit of information was collected, it was shared with the class.

By now the class had important knowledge of the township. At this point it would have been easy to quit. I was ready to quit. But my class' enthusiasm prompted me to continue working.

We now began to exhaust local sources of information, exploring township records, letters, old newspapers, diaries, and church records. We were beginning to build a good framework on which to write a book.

Then came the most exciting part of the project. In the summer of 1975, we began interviewing many residents of the community. These people were especially cooperative. At each interview, two students usually accompanied me. Questions and answers were recorded on tape.

Once the tapes were completed they had to be transcribed. All transcriptions were done by groups of students. Once the words were written on paper, they were then placed into subject areas such as, religion, education, geography, etc.

This class did an outstanding job. Wherever possible students were involved in making this product. It was their effort, enthusiasm, and hard work that brought this book about. To them I shall always be grateful.

Our township history is not complete. No doubt we have left out some information. As with any oral history, there are inaccuracies. However, we hope our work will serve as a basis of history for Lawrence Township.

I would like to thank all those who agreed to let us tape them. Without their cooperation, much information would have been left out; also Robert Miller and Robert Weidenfeld who edited this entire manuscript; Mrs. Marlene Rouse who not only proofread the material, but also helped to collect much of the information; and Barb Thomas and Judy Morris, seniors at Frontier High School, who typed this entire book.

Finally, this book is dedicated to the people of Lawrence Township. It is their story. Through their cooperation and willingness to contribute, this book has been written.

James Mahoney

"THE WILDERNESS THAT BECAME LAWRENCE"

The Eighth Grade Class

Christina Becker
Teresa Becker
Ted Bickish
Mark Binegar
Betty Brooks
Steve Brown
Ruth Cline
Ray Douglas
Debra Eddy
Jim Erb
Ron Graham
Bill Grosklos
Debbie Gutberlet

Doug Lamm
Brenda Leister
Vesta Minder
Debbie Morningstar
Marvin Mosser
Diane Myers
Bill Reed
Brian Rouse
Ken Starkey
Chris Strickler
Susan Sullivan
Anita Ward
Ron Wright
Mr. James Mahoney, Teacher

DID YOU KNOW?

. . .that Lawrence Township is the only geometrically square township in Washington County?

. . .that the first Children's Home in the state of Ohio was founded by Catherine Fay Ewing in Lawrence Township?

. . .that nearly 2,000 people lived on Cow Run at one time during the oil boom?

. . .that the original bid for the construction of Lawrence High School was $21,000?

. . .that 193 male citizens from Lawrence Township served in Civil War? Out of these, 20 died in serving with the Northern forces?

. . .that "Cow Run" derives its name from the fact the creek had many salt springs where milkmaids could usually find their cows. At that time the cows were not fenced in?

. . .that in the 19th Century the Board of Education in Lawrence Township set aside a special fund for establishing a college for the youth of the community?

. . .that Captain John Sharp, an early settler of Lawrence Township, led a company of men during the War of 1812? He was captured by the British, but escaped from a British ship?

. . .that the first industry in Lawrence Township was the manufacture of chestnut shingles?

. . .that Moss Run was once a station on the "Underground Railroad" helping Southern slaves escape North to freedom?

. . .that Bear Run derives its name from the fact a hunter named Archer met and defeated a bear in hand-to-paw combat?

. . .that the first store in Lawrence Township was opened by William Powell in 1838 in the upper part of the township, near the corner of Independence Township?

. . .that the first school in the township was opened in 1810 by a young Virginian just below the mouth of Cow Run?

. . .that according to the 1870 census Lawrence Township was the most populated township in Washington County? (with the exception of Marietta)

EARLY HISTORY AND SETTLEMENT

The early settlement of Lawrence was preceded by important events in the country. During the mid 1700's the French and English were both struggling for what is now Ohio. The Indians were in Ohio first and wanted to remain because of the abundant game, beautiful valleys, and good cultivating soil. Unfortunately for them, this was not to be their fate. Indian leaders such as Pontiac and Cornstalk did all they could, in vain, to prevent the white man's settlement. The whites wished to clear the land, start settlements, and bring civilization to the area.

After the colonists won independence, the Ordinance of 1787 was passed by Congress. This act paved the way for organization and settlement of the Northwest Territory, of which Ohio and Lawrence were a part. Later, five states were created out of the territory; namely, Ohio, Michigan, Indiana, Illinois, and Wisconsin. As part of this Ordinance, religion and civil liberty were guaranteed as well as educational opportunity. Perhaps Daniel Webster said it best, "I doubt whether one single lawmaker, ancient or modern, has produced effects of more distinct, marked or lasting character than the Ordinance of 1787." Marietta was the first settlement of the Northwest Territory. Later, in 1803, Ohio became a state by meeting the requirements of statehood under the Ordinance.

The hardships these first settlers had were many. Scarlet

fever, smallpox, securing game, and Indians were just a few.
Courage and perserverance seem almost inadequate words to
describe these early settlers. Indians were a constant threat
to settlers. There was a massacre at Big Bottom a part of what
is now Morgan County. There was also another noted attack
on settlers at Fort Frye. Certainly, there were many isolated
incidents.

Thaddeus Harris wrote in his journal of another peculiar
problem: "The vast flight of pigeons in this country seem
incredible. But, there is a large forest in Waterford, containing
several hundred acres, which has been killed in consequence
of their lighting upon it during the autumn of 1801. Such
numbers lodged upon the trees that they broke off large limbs;
and the ground below is covered. . .which has not only killed
all the undergrowth, but all the trees are dead as if they had
been girdled."

All of this information serves as a preface for the settling
of Lawrence Township.

"It is not definitely known who the first settler of
Lawrence was. The Dye family, the Hoff family, and the Chambers
family all made permanent improvements in the Little Muskingum
valley before 1810. As would be expected, the first settlers
chose the rich bottom land along the river, the more distant
terraces not being entered till comparatively recent times."

"John Dye and Samuel Dye emigrated from Virginia and settled
in the valley of the Little Muskingum, a short distance above
the mouth of Cow Run, in 1805. A few years later their father
John Dye, Sr., with the remainder of the family, settled in
the same neighborhood. John Dye, second, was born in New Jersey

in 1774. He emigrated with his family to Virginia, and then to Ohio, and settled in Lawrence Township. He was married to Hannah Hoff, who was born in 1774, and died in 1857. He died during the epidemic of 1823. They had eleven children: Enoch, who died at the age of 20; Thomas, Mophet, Susan, wife of Robert Pierce, Eliza, wife of Nathan Davis; Samuel, second, esq., Emma, wife of William Chambers; Daniel, John W.; A. Jackson, and Hannah, wife of George Cassady."

"A. Jackson Dye, son of John Dye, Jr., was born in 1816, in Lawrence Township. In 1838 he married Maria Petty, who was born in 1818. His family consisted of nine children: D. H., L. P., P. C., G. P., William A., H. M., wife of Gideon Campbell; S. A., Lattie and Emma.

"Graves of Samuel and Anna Dye,
early settlers of Lawrence."

"Samuel Dye, brother of John Dye, Jr., is well remembered by the older citizens of the township. He emigrated from Virginia and began life among the wooded hills of Lawrence in 1805. He died in 1860 at the age of 81. Susan Hoff, his wife, was born in Virginia in 1776 and died in 1849. The family consisted of ten children: John H., the oldest, was born in Virginia, in 1799 In 1822 he married Eliza O'Bleness, who was born in New York in 1803. The remaining children of Samuel Dye were: Hannah, first wife of Joseph Caywood; Sophia, wife of William Templeton, and afterwards of William McGee; Jonathon and James H., of Marietta; Nancy, wife of John R. Hill of Newport Township; and George, deceased. Hannah and Sophia married cousins of their father; Betsy and Mary were second cousins."

"When Samuel and John Dye settled in Lawrence Township, the nearest post office was Marietta, and the tract of country toward the north was an unbroken wilderness. The native animals of the forest nightly visited the improvement in search of prey. Domestic animals were in constant danger, and even children were unsafe beyond sight of the cabin."

"In dry weather the nearest mill was at Devol's Dam, 12 miles away, which could only be reached by traversing a cow path through the woods."

"Samuel Dye was a man of eccentric appearance. In cold weather a long cloak, covered with shorter capes (the number depending on the temperature) protected his tall and corpulent body. He was always in a good humor and called everybody "bub", which gave him the nickname "bub Sam". The electors of his township made him justice of the peace for 31 consecutive years.

4

The brothers and sisters of John and Samuel Dye were: Jane, wife of Henry Chamberlain; Polly, wife of James Hoff; Ezekiel and Jonathon, farmers of Lawrence Township; Bettie; Sallie, wife first of Thomas Worthington, then of John Cadwell, of Marietta Township; and Amos, a farmer and one of the early millers of Lawrence."

"Two sons of Jonathon Dye, Sr., were the victims of fatal accidents. Amos, died from the effect of a falling limb striking him on the head. The accident which resulted in the death of Alexander even more horrible. In 1873, during the oil excitement at Cow Run, Alexander's son, a small boy, found a can of fluid which his parents supposed to be refined coal oil. The lamp, which was more than half full of crude oil, was filled with what was supposed to be the superior article, and the evening was spent as usual around the open hearth. The lamp was noticed to flicker now and then, but no apprehension was excited. Before retiring, it was turned down and left burning on the table. Soon after retiring the flickering became more frequent and excited the fears of Mrs. Dye, who asked her husband to blow out the light. He hurried to obey the request, but when he picked up the lamp the flickering became frequent and more intense. Just as he was in the act of pitching the dangerous bowl from the cabin, the explosion of the half pint of nitro-glycerine which it contained-filled the air with small particles of the body of its victim, left the cabin in ruins and wounded every member of the family except the baby."

"Mrs. Abigal Dye, wife of Jonathon T. Dye, who was born in 1835 and died in 1878, is the daughter of James Jamison, who was born in Pennsylvania in 1795, and settled in Washington

County, in Liberty Township. Mr. Jamison was married to
Elizabeth Gordon, who was born in 1803 and died 1866. The
surviving members of the family are: Elizabeth, wife of
William Mosburgh, of Kansas; John H.; James M.; Mark B.;
Susan, wife of John Phunister; Rebecca, wife of Earstus Magee;
and Abigal."

"Diarca A. Dye, son of John H. Dye, was born in 1840. In
1860, he married Mary E. Clagston, who was born in Marietta
in 1840. They had six children. Dye went into the oil business
in 1862, and continued to operate wells until 1875, when he engaged
in the lumber business."

"Dr. William L. McCowan was born in Philadelphia in 1815,
and came to Ohio in 1846, stopping for a time at Harmar,
and eventually locating in this township at Morse Run, where
he has been postmaster since 1862. By his first wife, Marinda
J. Matthews, who died in 1870, he had ten children of whom eight
were: Elizabeth, Harriet (Bab), Marinda (Dye), Asa, Nancy H. (Dye),
William H., and Edward. By his second wife Dr. McCowan had
two children, Emma and Viola."

"One of the early, and possibly the first, settlers
of Lawrence Township, was John Chambers, who was born in
County Down, Ireland. He emigrated to America in 1798 and
settled in Lawrence Township about 1799. He settled at the
mouth of Chambers' Run, a short distance below and opposite
the mouth of Cow Run. From the time of his arrival in Ohio,
until he settled in Lawrence, he lived at the mouth of Wingett's
Run, in Ludlow Township. He built the first sawmill in the
township, on the Little Muskingum at the mouth of Chambers' Run.
His wife, Annie Greet, was a Scotch lady. It was chiefly through

6

Mr. Chambers' benevolence and influence that the Little Muskingum Church was built. He died in 1823."

"William Chambers, an older brother, settled in Lawrence on the farm opposite the mouth of Chambers' Run about 1810. A younger sister, who emigrated from Ireland at the same time, was the wife of Hugh Wilson, of Aurelius Township."

"James P., a son of William Chambers, was a natural land surveyor. Without the aid of an instrument he could run lines and measure land with remarkable accuracy."

"James G., the oldest son of John Chambers, was distinguished for two traits of character: fine social qualities and an uncontrollable temper. When in a fit of passion, his swearing was shocking. William, a younger brother, was killed by lightning at the age of seventeen. Joseph Chambers was a farmer and carpenter who lived on the east side of the Little Muskingum until 1850, when he moved to Marietta. He married Matilda McElhinney."

"Joseph Caywood settled about one mile below and opposite the mouth of Cow Run in 1806. His nephew Joseph, a son of William Caywood, settled in Lawrence. He was a leading member of the Presbyterian Church."

"About 1805 the Hoff family, consisting of Susan Hoff, the widow of Daniel Hoff, and seven children, four sons and three daughters, came from Alexandria, Virginia, and settled in Lawrence Township, above the mouth of Cow Run. Enoch Hoff, the oldest, had been a slave master and trader. He settled near the mouth of Morse Run (Moss Run). He was married five times. The children by his third wife were: James P; Angeline and Mary. Both James P. and his father were known in the community as "nigger catchers." Refugee slaves on several occasions were induced into the Hoff residence, and there they were captured and carried back to bondage."

"Hannah Hoff married John Dye. Jonathan married Betsy Duncan and settled on Duck Creek."

"William Hoff was born in old Virginia in 1780, and settled in Lawrence Township, where he died in 1844. His wife, Elizabeth Dutton, born in 1785, died in 1839. Of their children, Daniel died in Iowa; Margaret resided in Lawrence; Alfred, in Muskingum Township; Lida died in Lawrence Township; George is in Illinois, and Amos is in Iowa. Alfred established a woolen mill at Marietta. Susan was the wife of Samuel Dye. Polly married Isaac Hill, and moved to Hocking River. James, the youngest of the family, married three times, and had five sons and eleven daughters."

"John Sharp, well-known all over the county as associate judge common pleas, was born in Pennsylvania in 1771, and came to Ohio about 1800. He made an improvement on the east side of the Little Muskingum near the Newport Township line. The first orchard on the Little Muskingum was planted by him. He was very large, corpulent man, and was looked upon as the solon of the community. He served as judge of common pleas several years, and a few days before his death in 1823, was commissioned judge of the superior court. His wife, whose maiden name was Mary Mitchell, and ten children survived him."

"About the year 1812 Nathan Matheney (originally spelled Metheny), a native of Virginia, came from Athens County, Ohio, and settled above and opposite the mouth of Fifteen Creek. He had, by his first wife, Elizabeth Everly, eight children; by his second, Barbara Fultz, two; by his third wife, Katie Farley,

six. All but one of these 16 children settled in Lawrence
Township. Noah, the oldest, made the first improvement on Bear
Run."

"George Templeton, Esq., came to Lawrence Township from
Newport, and made an improvement on the Little Muskingum
about two miles above the mouth of Fifteen, in 1819. He
served as justice of the peace in Lawrence for 33 years. In
partnership with Beniah Snodgrass and Benjamin Burres, he built
a saw-mill in 1834, about one mile further up the river. He
died about 1850. He was the father of twelve children.
His son William was killed by accident. Joseph settled on Bear
Run. James settled on Fifteen Creek. Let it, was the main support
of the Lawrence Baptist Church."

"Zeptha Treadway was one of the earliest settlers of the
upper part of the township. About 1820 he came from New Jersey,
and entered land below and opposite the mouth of Archer's Fork.
He had two sons: Jonathon, who settled near the same place, and
the other Jerre, who was a self-constituted preacher in the
county infirmary."

"Every royal household has its jester, every circus a clown,
and no community is complete without a professional story
teller. Lawrence, in the person of Jacob Bartmess, possessed
a Munchausen in whom was combined the cunning of a wit and the
oddity of a genius. "Jake" lived in a cabin on the east side of
the Little Muskingum, nearly opposite the Baptist Church, as early
as 1825. He cared nothing about domestic affairs, and was happy
only when tramping the woods with his gun on his shoulder, or
entertaining his neighbors with the story of the mighty deeds of
"my brother George." George was always the hero of his blood chill-

ing stories. A few peculiarities of the house are worthy of mention. The black-eyed children had a terror of strangers. A rustle of bare feet followed a rap on the door, and the entering visitor could see nothing of children save several pairs of sparkling black eyes peering from under the bed. When the boys grew older, they were given an outfit of buckskin pantaloons. Although the boys were growing longer, the pantaloons from time to time became shorter, they being Jake's only recourse for thongs. He died on a hunting expedition down the river near Cairo, in 1876, aged 77 years."

"Hiram Snodgrass emigrated from Bull Creek, West Virginia, and settled on Bear Run in Lawrence Township, in 1812. He died on the same place in 1879. His wife's maiden name was Drucilla Oliver. Eli Snodgrass, a brother of Hiram, and husband of Polly Templeton, was one of the early settlers of Lawrence. Beniah Snodgrass is well remembered by all the old settlers of Lawrence.. He was married twice, first to Anna McKibban and then to Julia Anne Clark. He settled in section ten, and in partnership with Burris & Templeton, built the Templeton Mill in 1834."

"Lucas Cassady settled in Lawrence Township, about one mile below the mouth of Fifteen, in 1821. He continued to reside in Lawrence Township until 1850, when he was killed by accident in Maysville, Kentucky. His family consisted of three sons and one daughter. Marton settled opposite Painter Run; George at the head of Morse (Moss) Run, and William J. on Morse (Moss) Run. Diadamia was married to Samuel Dye, third, from whom she was afterwards divorced, and married to Carlton Palmer, of Newport Township."

. . "Joe Harris, who settled near the mouth of Morse Run

(Moss Run) in 1825, was the hero of the woods. In manners he was somewhat rough, but possessed a kind heart and accommodating disposition. He was a useful man in the clearing, and could always be relied upon at a raising."

"The mill at the mouth of Fifteen was owned by George W. Reynolds in 1830. It came into possession of Charles Akinson in 1836. Charles was a grandson of Cornelius Akinson, who was wounded seven times in one battle in the Revolution. Charles was born on the Juniata in 1796, and in early life learned milking and boat-building. His death occurred in Marietta in 1880. William, his oldest son, made an improvement on Bear Run in 1838. His first wife was Jane Templeton, daughter of Squire Templeton. He married for his second wife Theda Patterson, sister of Dr. Patterson, a prominent man in the community."

"In the autumn of 1832, Joseph McElhinney and his only sister Anne, came from the north of Ireland and settled on the Little Muskingum, a short distance above and opposite the mouth of Elk Run. He found there a clearing of six acres and a small orchard and cabin which had been made by Jacob Newlin some 12 years previous. John McElhinney died in 1874, in his 80th year."

. ."John Rake made the first improvement on section six. He sold to A. Campbell and Samuel Bush, and purchased the McAllister improvement in 1835. He died opposite the mouth of Bear Run in 1875."

"Solomon Tice, an early settler of Ludlow Township, pushed into Lawrence Township in the pursuit of his ambition to suddenly make a great fortune. At the mouth of a small stream emptying into the Little Muskingum, the "Governor," as he was nicknamed, discovered a composite rock which he supposed to contain silver. As early as 1825 he bored a well on Fifteen Creek, opposite the mouth of Mill Fork, to the depth of 300 feet, in search of salt. His tools were inadequate to the further progress of the work, and the attempt was abandoned. It is said that his confidence of obtaining a productive salt well was broken by the appearance, at the depth of 200 feet, of a black, greasy liquid, which later investigations proved to have been oil."

"Archibald Campbell settled in the northeast corner of Lawrence Township in 1833. He was born in Pennsylvania in 1806, and married Hannah Sample, who was born in 1820. Mr. Campbell was the first postmaster of Lawrence Post Office."

. . ."The first store in Lawrence Township was opened by William Powell in 1838, in the upper part of the township, near the corner of Independence. He removed from Lawrence to Grand View Township, where he engaged in the practice of medicine."

"John Barnhart was one of the early settlers of the upper corner of the township. He was a nervous and superstitious character, who was in constant dread of ghosts. One night, while passing through a clearing, a man witho a head appeared, and in a few days it was announced that Barnhart had died of nervous prostration."

"In 1840, Major Issac M. Hannold removed to this county and purchased a farm eight miles from Marietta, in Lawrence Township, on the ridge between Duck Creek and Little Muskingum. He was for four years superintendent of the infirmary, and was one of the partners in the Old Elm Well, the second producing oil well on Cow Run. In 1865 he removed to Monitor, Indiana, where he died in 1867, two years after the death of his wife."

"We have now given a sketch of the best known of the early settlers along the Muskingum Valley. The large tract of territory at the head of Fifteen Creek was settled mostly by Scotch families who came to this county between 1840 and 1850. They are an intelligent and industrious class of people, and have contributed largely toward the wealth of the county. Wool growing was the predominant industry of the Scotch communities."

"George Heslop was born in England in 1790. He emigrated to America and settled in Lawrence Township in 1844. His death occurred in 1878. Agnes Dixon, his wife, was born in 1794, and died in 1840.. . .His son, John Heslop came from England in 1844, and settled on 140 acres of land in the north part of Lawrence Township."

"Ralph Cuthbert emigrated from England, where he was a master shepherd, in 1842. He settled in Lawrence Township, on Fifteen Creek, and engaged in general farming and wool growing.."

. . . ."John Slobaum was the first German settler on the highlands in the northwest part of the township, known as German Ridge. He entered land and made an improvement previous to 1840. This ridge was settled by people of German descent."

"John D. Pape, Sr., born in Hanover, Germany, in 1874, emigrated to this country in 1838, came to Washington County, and settled in Lawrence Township, where he died. . . .In 1812 John D. Pape served in Bonaparte's army."

". . John Q. Pepper settled in Lawrence Township in 1853, having emigrated from Virginia. He married Olive Maxon, who was born in 1822. They had eight children."

". . The most rapid growth of population was between 1863 and 1870, caused by the extensive production of oil within that period."

"Eldridge G. Gilbert was born in Massachusetts in 1828, emigrated to Aurelius township, Washington County, in 1858, and to Cow Run, Lawrence Township, in 1864, where he built a machine shop. His wife, Mary A. Davis, was born in 1840, in Adams Township. They have a family of three children: Juna B., born in 1870; Laura M., in 1874 and Ethel S., in 1879."

"Victor Torner was born in Europe in 1815 and emigrated to Virginia, and in 1861 settled in Belpre Township, afterwards coming to Lawrence, where he was superintendent of the Exchange Companies oil wells. He built the flouring mill at Newport. In 1848 he married Charlotta G. Weiss, who was born in 1819. They had three children: Elvira, wife of J. R. Dye; Hugo T., and William V."

"Alfred Hoff was born in Lawrence Township, Washington County, June 24, 1817. He was married in 1839 to Miss Mary N. Atkinson, who died in the same year. In 1840 he was married a second time, to Miss Elizabeth Fuller. Eight children have been born of this marriage. Mr. Hoff was for twenty-five years chief engineer on boats on the Ohio, its tributaries, and on southern rivers. When the Civil War broke out he was in the south, and immediately after the fall of Sumter transported two confederate regiments from Arkansas to New Orleans. Not relishing such work, he immediately set out for home. On his arrival, he with two others chartered a boat and took out the first troops that left Ohio. He served throughout the whole war."

"In 1868 George E. Lehmer emigrated to Lawrence from Pennsylvania, in which state he was born in 1837. He married Annie E. Stickle, who was born in 1840. To Mr. and Mrs. Lehmer has been born one son, Willie H. In 1873 Mr. Lehmer was elected to the office of school director.

He had charge of six oil wells, which produced about five barrels per day. While serving in Company F of the Pennsylvania Reserves he was wounded at Antietam and also at Fredericksburgh."

"W. Strachan was born in England in 1831. He came to America in 1843, and remained in Allegheny County, Pennsylvania, until 1860, when he came to Cow Run and engaged in the oil business. He was Justice of the Peace for 9 years. He married Sarah Johnson, of this township, and a granddaughter of Alderman Johnson, an early settler of this township, and daughter of Edward Johnson. They had five children: David, Mary Margaret, Sarah and Edward."[1]

The preceding section was taken from William's History of Washington County, Ohio. We have reprinted it for the posterity of Lawrence Township. It should also serve very helpful for those who are interested in tracing their family trees.

As one can easily see, the early settlers of Lawrence came from a wide variety of places and backgrounds. Some of the early marriages in the township are listed below as taken from Washington County Probate Court Records and compiled by Mrs. John Doak.

Martha Amlin (Marietta)--William Hill, Jr., (Law)
    January 31, 1822.

John Bartmess--Margaret Snodgrass (Law)
    November 2, 1820.

Joseph Caywood--(Fearing)--Hannah Dye (Law)
    April 14, 1822.

James Covey (Law)--Eliza Wells (Salem)
    February 2, 1819.

Susan Dye--Robert Pierce (Law)
    December 2, 1819.

Jane Greggs (Marietta)--James Hoff (Law)
    March 4, 1824.

Eunice Henear--Jonas Main (Law)
    November 3, 1816.

Betsy Johnson--Reuben Williams (Law)
    April 17, 1823.

Polly Lowe (Fearing)--Alderman Johnson (Law)
    March 9, 1819.

Rebecca Cook (Fearing)--Elisha Rose (Law)
    April 27, 1817.

Letty McKibben--Henry O'Blenniss (Law)
    November 27, 1821.

Rachel Parker--Elisha Ryan (Law)
    August 14, 1821.

Louisa Posey (Marietta)--William McKibbon (Law)
    August 13, 1826.

James Rayner--Nancy Mitchen (Law)
    January 2, 1820.

Many of these marriages produced offspring whose relatives
today still live in Lawrence.

Miss Eliza Brooks, a teacher at Lawrence Elementary School
for 33 years, did a considerable amount of research on the
township. Miss Brooks, who taught school for 51 years, retired
in 1971. Until the time of her death she could recall all her
former students, tell who they had married, and very likely

the names of their children. She never married to have her own children, so nieces and nephews had to suffice. Later it was great nieces and nephews. She never forgot a birthday. She died September 23, 1974, and on a beautiful day was laid to rest on top of one of the hills she loved in the Moss Run Cemetery. The information she collected was passed on by her sister, Mrs. Lulu Root. We are extremely grateful Miss Brooks had given her time and effort to preserve the history of the township.

"Some of the prominent residents who are descendants of the early settlers are George Hoff, who married Katie Morningstar, and had a son, Walter. James and Mary Hadley are the children of the late W. L. Hadley. Grant Rake married Emma McFarland in 1887. They raised a fine family consisting of Ada, Bernard, John, Mansel, and Mrs. Grace Kesselring. Mr. and Mrs. Loss Rake are the parents of Wilbur, Guy, and Gale Rake. Mr. J. L. Clark married Lou Davis, the parents of Mrs. Ruth McGregor and Mrs. Audrey DeLong. Mr. Clark married for his second, wife, Mrs. Elizabeth Masters Starkey, and they have a son, John and a daughter, Virginia, who is a trained nurse."

"Mr. and Mrs. William DePuy are the parents of two sons, Arthur, deceased, and Floyd who married Mary Bowersock and have a son, Gale. Mrs. Jane Henning Bohlen, widow of the late Samuel Bohlen, is the mother of Annie DePuy and William Bohlen, who married Ada Reed. Their children are Wilbur and Dorothy. Mrs. Martha DePuy, widow of Squire A. DePuy lives at Steel Run. Mr. and Mrs. A. DePuy are the parents of A. J., who married Alice Grudier; William married Annie Bohlen; Emily married George Reed."

17

"Mr. and Mrs. Harvey Thomas are the parents of Effie, who married Frank Edgar; Dorothy, who married a Warren; John who married Gladys Biehl, and Edwin."

"Wilson Martin, who married Martha Joy, had the following children: Annie Rutherford, Mae Biehl, Irene Hanna, Mildred Lane, and two sons, Harvey, who married Gladys Rutherford, and Charles, who married Myrna King."

"James Martin is the father of Mrs. Lillie King Mosser and Mrs. Rutherford. Mrs. Martin died when the girls were small and they were cared for by their aunt, Mrs. Ella Whitney."

"George Martin married a Miss Joy and they had three sons, Edward, who married Sylvia Hearn, Guy, who married Leona Brookover, and Gale, who married Goldie Hearn."

"Mr. and Mrs. Thomas McGregor have lived their entire lives at Moss Run. Their children are Agnes, Jessie and Curtis. Curtis is survived by his widow, Mrs. Nellie Ridgway McGregor, and six children, Geraldine, Gerald, Carrol, Richard, Josephine, and Mary Kathryn."

"Mr. and Mrs. Delbert Biehl operated a grocery store at Moss Run. Their four children are Duane, Cecil, Richard and James."

"Mr. and Mrs. Sherman Dye lived at Moss Run. Their two children are: Chester of Iowa, and Mrs. Edna Boyd Buell of Newport Pike."

"Mr. and Mrs. A. L. Root are living in the Gracey neighborhood and their children are Bradley, who married Esther Hill and lives in Pennsylvania: Mrs. Letha Athey, Mrs. Joseph Semon, and Bernard, who married Lulu Brooks."

"Mr. and Mrs. Simeon Miller are the parents of Dean and Floyd who live in Cow Run community."

"Mr. and Mrs. Russel Ridgway are the parents of Hayden who married Anna Loughlin, Mrs. Edward Patterson, Mrs. Nellie McGregor, and James, who married Miss Opal Strickler."

"Mr. and Mrs. Walter LaFaber are the parents of Roe Hill LaFaber, who married Mildred Lane, and Ronald, who married Ruth Scott. Roe's children are Calvin and Carol. Ronald's daughter is Patricia. Lewis Morgenstern married Bessie Whiston and their children are Ione and Lewis Jr."

"Mr. Edward Lane married Minnie Ewing and their children are Mrs. Mildred LaFaber, Margaret, Mary and Norman."

"Mr. Virgil Baker is a son of the late David Baker. Virgil's wife is Freda Hune and their two children are Richard and Norma Jean."

"Mr. and Mrs. John Whitney have three daughters; Lora, Edna and Opal."

"The late William Huntsman and his surviving wife had the following children: Edna Forshey, Pearl Heldman, Floyd, Glenn, and Harley."[2]

Hopefully, Miss Brooks' research, along with William's History, will give our readers a good background of the many families of Lawrence Township. Some of the research done by Miss Brooks may be inaccurate in light of deaths, divorces, new babies, etc. It is not our intent to try to include all the families of Lawrence. We have simply compiled others research and added it to our history. Our intent, rather, has been to try to fill in some of the gaps in the Lawrence history in hopes of preserving it. Most of our research in doing this consisted of talking to older citizens of the community about the past.

The next part includes research supplied by Jerry Devol on the postal history of Lawrence.

The first post office in the township was established on December 20, 1833, and was given the name of Lawrence. It was located on the farm of John W. Dye in the central portion of the township. The Lawrence Post Office was discontinued in 1843. The post office was re-established in Lawrence in 1846 with Archibald Campbell as postmaster. The office was moved in 1849 to William Hune's log store, where Alexander Clark served as postmaster. Clark died in 1865 and the office was moved to Independence Township. In 1893, the post office was moved back to the Hune Store, where William Hune's daughter, Carrie, served as postmaster. It remained there until 1912 when the store closed permanently.[3]

The second post office in the township was established in 1846 at the home of Joseph Caywood in the southwestern part of the township. It was designated "Lower Lawrence Post Offce." William Caywood took charge in 1859 followed by William Guyton in 1863. In 1864, the office was moved to George Robinson's grist mill. The office was discontinued in 1867.[4]

Kinnard Barrackman was the first postmaster to serve at the Moss Run Post Office, established in 1857. In 1863, the office was moved to the store of "McCowan and Sons." The office remained here until 1917, with the exception of one brief period when it was moved to nearby Shreve's Store. In 1917, patrons were served from Marietta by rural free delivery. Arthur "Windy" Lane and Curtis McGregor were rural carriers to Moss Run for many years.[5]

The Cow Run Post Office was opened November 4, 1869, in the store of William Guittean. John Campbell purchased Guittean's general store in 1871 and was named second postmaster. In 1874, "Connor & Harvey" bought the store and had the office there until 1884, when it was destroyed by fire. Many postmasters served in Cow Run after this, with the last one being Anna Miller in her store until 1916.[6]

Steel Run Post Office was opened in 1878 just above where Dart is now. It was in the country store of Clinton DePuy and Jas. Greene. In 1891, the office was moved to the home of Anson S. DePuy. It moved several more times until 1906 when George Reed became postmaster in his store. The office was closed in 1918.[7]

Heslop Post Office was established in 1880 in northwestern Lawrence, named after the Heslop family that settled there. It was first located in Alla Winsor's general store. "Winsor & Grass" also manufactured stogies. This store burned down in 1889. From that point, the post office was located for short times in several area stores. Some of these stores were owned by Dixon Heslop, Ed Kitts, and George Hewson. The post office was closed in 1923.[8]

Another post office in the oil region of southern Lawrence was "Gracie Post Office" established in 1882 with William Gracie as postmaster. Henry Scott became the new postmaster in 1885 and had a store there also. It was finally sold to William Roat in 1895 where the post office remained until the store's discontinuance in 1916.[9]

Dye Post Office was established in 1883 to serve residents in the northwest on Pleasant Ridge.[10]

Fay Post Office was established on Bear Run in 1887 in honor of Rev. Levi Fay. This post office was always in the same building until its end in 1936. Several people were combined storekeepers and postmasters, most notably the McCauley Brothers.[11]

Sitka had a small post office beginning in 1890 in Luther Hill's Store. It was discontinued in 1916.[12]

This brings us to the only post office left in the township. That is the Dart Post Office originally established by Samuel Bohlen in 1905, at his store where Dart is now. Today, Dean Eddy serves as postmaster and has since 1959.[13]

Two students, Susan Sullivan and Steve Brown, with myself spent an evening talking with Mrs. June Hendershot, a former teacher who has done much research of Lawrence Township. Presently, she lives in the extreme northeastern part of the township. Her home was once a wayside inn, serving as a stopping point for weary travelers and a selling place for peddlers. In addition, there was a livery barn close by. The inn, which provided room and board, formerly belonged to the William Hune family.

"June's home was once a wayside inn."

A covered bridge stands close by named after Mr. Hune. The
bridge was built about 1877 by Rollan Meredith of Marietta. At
one time in this part of the township there existed a settlement
named Lawrence.

"Hune Bridge"

Some of the first to settle it were Jesse Fleming and Vachel
Dickerson, an associate of Lewis Wetzell. The Hune family built
the major portion of town. William Hune built a blacksmith
shop, a saw mill, a grist mill, a tobacco packing house, and
a sorghum making factory. In additon to this, there was an old
log church. Mr. Hune's operations employed many people. No one
we talked to seemed to know why the town died out or exactly when.
In 1942, much of the property that once contained this town was
purchased by Otto Heldman, June's father. At that time, nothing
was left with the exception of their house.[14]

Another group we talked to was the Senior Citizens of Lawrence.
Two students, Ron Graham and Teresa Becker, and myself spent an
afternoon talking to Bernice Farley, Mildred LaFaber, and Fay

Farley. Their group was organized in 1970 by Bernice Farley with the purpose of getting elderly citizens together for recreation. As of this writing, there are 13 active members, three of them being male. All members are over 50 years of age. Mildred LaFaber's father was Ed Lane, who was a wholesale butcher in Lawrence from approximately 1902 until 1930. He would butcher cows, hogs, pigs, and sheep, and then take the meat to Marietta for sale. Before taking livestock to Ed Lane, people would go to Elic Smith to have their livestock weighed, because he was one of the few people who had a set of scales.[15]

Probably one of the most familiar landmarks to the people of Lawrence is Pete Baker Hill, which really isn't in Lawrence. Located on Route 26 between Marietta and Lawrence, only the bottom of the hill is in Lawrence Township. The Senior Citizens told us that around the turn of the century there was a hotel located at the bottom of the hill, owned and run by Pete Baker. It served as a stopping place between Marietta and Lawrence, used especially by wagon drivers bringing oil from Lawrence to Marietta. They told us that about 1917 the hotel burned down.[16]

One of the most interesting items the ladies told us about was the Cow Run Concert Band. It was the pride of the community for many years. The band built a hall on Cow Run for many social events. It was here that, in addition to concerts, the band sponsored silent movies. (On one occasion the movie projector caught fire.) The band played at local celebrations, picnics, and many other social gatherings. Almost every Saturday, there was something going on in the community. The most probable reason the band ended was members were busy with many other things and gradually just quit.[17]

(We have included an old post card of the band. Some of the identified members are Ed Becker, Frank Weinstock, Ray Bush, Bernard Bush, Harry Bush, George Smith, Frank Campbell, Henry Wallace, Ed Patterson, Ed Lauer, and Willie Biehl. Frank Smith was the leader.)

"COW RUN CONCERT BAND"

"COW RUN CONCERT BAND"

There were many other social occasions for Lawrence citizens during the early 1900's. People would get together to make cider, husk corn, peel apples, quilt, raise barns, chop wood, and many other things. The purpose was to mix work with fun. For example, Moss Run had an early baseball team.[4] There was a ball field on the Glen and Willie Biehl farm. Also, Square dances were often held in Moss Run.

According to Elmer Miller, owner of Miller's Store on Route 26 near Dart, during the early 1900's people just seemed to help people more. There were many types of "frolics", where people got together to do some sort of work, such as "wood frolics". Here, people would cut firewood for everyone.[18]

Of course, not all the recreation of the 1900's was work mixed with pleasure. Ray Douglas and Bill Grosklos, two of my students, and I talked to Reed Hanna and Walter Hoff about some other things last winter. They told us about the "Quail House" run by Anne Masters and her daughters sometime in the 1890's. It seems the Quail House was quite a popular tavern during the times. It was located across from where the Grange Hall is today. In addition to this, over the years there were several "bootleggin" establishments.[19]

Any history of a community is not without its tragic incidents and unusual circumstances. "In 1839, Elisha Rose, a well known citizen of Newport Township, engaged in a horse race with a man named Hinkel, on the banks of the Little Muskingum near the mouth of Archer's Fork, which proved fatal to his life. A purse of three dollars was put up and the contestants started the race. When Rose reached the end, he arose in his saddle and looked for his opponent. The horse at that moment stumbled and pitched the rider against a rock. Rose died in a few days from the wound, and his estate received the purse."

"In 1859, Porter Flint and one of the Mitchell boys were drowned in the Little Muskingum at Proute's mill. A raft which they were floating became unmanageable at the mill dam, and both were thrown into the stream."

"The most abhorrent of the many cases of drowning in the township occurred at Cow Run. A daughter of one of the workmen one day went to start a fire. While she was stooping over the top of the tank, her foothold gave away, and she was taken from the reservoir in a lifeless condition."[20]

One of the most recent drowning tragedies took place in 1973. A boy scout group from Woodsfield capsized on the Little Muskingum near Dart while on a camping expedition. One scout drowned. His body was not found for two weeks.

From the many people we talked to, it becomes clear the stories of some of the most disastrous floods. The Little Muskingum and its creeks still flood the banks. Probably the most talked about flood was the one of 1898. Destroyed was a drilling well located against the hill upon Fifteen Creek. The stem of the well landed a good mile from the mouth of Fifteen Creek, and the cullwheels and cables were strung down the creek in the willows. The flood also took a store owned by Ed Kitz.[8] It seems everything on Fifteen was destroyed with the exception of one house owned by a man named Stricker. It was saved perhaps because both doors were opened at each end of the house. The house also had a big chimney and strong foundation. It seems also a church was uprooted and, from a hill people saw it speeding down the creek with its bell ringing.[21] There were others especially bad floods in 1896, 1913 and 1973.

"Today the Little Muskingum floods."

Floods were not the only tragic incidents. Several twisters destroyed property in Lawrence. Diseases and viruses often caused many deaths.

Veterans from Lawrence have served in every war our country has fought. At one time, O. S. Reed was one of the oldest living veterans of the Civil War. He was 99 when he died. We have included a copy of his discharge of 1865. Reed served three years during the Civil War and was with General Sherman on his march from Atlanta to the sea. He also served many years as an elected township official.

Ron Graham and Brian Rouse spent a considerable amount of time researching one of Ohio's most famous scouts, Lewis Wetzell. His home, near Wheeling, West Virginia, was attacked by Indians when he was a small boy. All members of his family except Lewis and a brother were killed. From this point, Indians were to be Wetzell's lifelong enemy.

28

Lewis Wetzell was born in 1763. He died in 1808 and today his remains are in Moundsville, West Virginia. Many a story has been told of Wetzell's daring escapades. Wetzell spent a great deal of time on the Ohio and Little Muskingum Rivers between Fort McHenry (Wheeling) and Fort Harmar (Marietta). It was at those times that Wetzell passed through what is now Lawrence.

On one occasion Lewis was out chopping wood. He looked up and saw six Indians staring at him. The Indians wanted Lewis to go with them. He told them he needed to split logs first. He drove a wedge into the tree and told the Indians he could finish quicker if they would help him. They readily agreed and Lewis told them to stick their hands in the crevasse produced by the wedge and pull. When they did this, Lewis, with one swing of the ax, knocked the wedge out and it caught the Indians' hands in a vise. Lewis then made short work of the Indians with the ax by scalping all six of them.[22]

From the Marietta Times comes another interesting account. It seems General Josia Harmar of Fort Harmar started a program in 1785 with the Indians that assured safety from his army in return for friendly relations. Wetzell happened to be in the area at the time. As he left Fort Harmar, he is said to have shot a Delaware Indian sitting on his pony. Efforts were made to capture Wetzell, but he had too many friends in the area to allow him to be caught.

Mrs. Hendershot gave an undated account of Wetzell from the Marietta times. There is a cave where Wetzell is said to have hidden overlooking Lawrence Township Route 584 and the Little Muskingum River. It is reached by turning right off Route 26 near

29

Moss Run. In the spring of 1975, I took a group of students
to find the cave. We are sure we found the described cave and
took a picture of it. The cover of our book is a picture
of the Little Muskingum, taken from the cave.

"This is the cave where Wetzell is to
have stayed in Lawrence."

The cave would have been an excellent spot for viewing Indians
on the Little Muskingum.

Finally, Wetzell employed a trick that made him famous. He
would put his hat on a stick and hold it around a tree so Indians
would fire at the hat, thinking it to be him.

It's important to mention the many fine doctors who served
the community over the years. These early doctors had difficult
times in trying to see patients due mainly to transportation problems.

Homemade remedies sufficed for most less serious illnesses. For
the most part these remedies proved to be very helpful. However,
some remedies were much worse than the sickness. One remedy told
us was the cure for "tired blood". For its cure you only needed
to cut the bark of a wild cherry tree and let it set in water

a day or two before drinking. The cure for diarrhea was very similar. You followed the same procedure only using the bark of a sycamore tree.[23]

The first professional practitioner in the township was Dr. Tyler, who maintained an office above the mouth of Fifteen in 1839.[24]

Other doctors who practiced in the community in the Nineteenth Century days were Joshua Rogers, William Puterson, and George Fleming.

Of special mention are Doctors William McCowan and James McCowan. William McCowan originally came from Philadelphia. He was extremely well liked, enjoying the confidence of the community. He died in 1890 of cancer.

Dr. Jim McCowan was the grandson of William McCowan. He is especially remembered by older citizens of the community as being an exceptional pediatrician. His office was near Cow Run. One story Nellie Rake told us about him concerned a small boy's inquisitiveness concerning the birth of babies. Not being able to put him off, Dr. McCowan finally told him that babies were hatched in bottles by hens. So, naturally the boy, wanting to witness such a wonder, carried out perfectly the doctor's instructions. Day after day he checked the bottle. Finally, in anger he jerked the cork off the bottle and took it back to the doctor. The doctor not to be outdone, told him the reason the baby didn't hatch was because the boy had pulled the cork. Dr. McCowan finished his practice at Marietta in the 1950's.

31

"Doctor McCowan"

Certainly many changes have occurred in the township over the years. We've left the story of the oil boom to another chapter. Most of the people in the township today work in surrounding areas. A 15 minute drive on State Route 26 to Marietta is a far cry from the eight-hour trip during horse and wagon days.

It would be impossible for us to be inclusive of all the history of Lawrence. Perhaps we shall add to it at another time. Instead, we have presented as near accurate overview of the township's early settlement and history as we could. We hope this chapter has served as a tribute to the many brave pioneers of Lawrence.

To all whom it may Concern.

Know ye, That _Christian S. Reed_ a _Corporal_ of Captain _Albert G. Kates_ Company, (_K_) _92_ Regiment of _Ohio Foot_ VOLUNTEERS, who was enrolled on the _Eighteenth_ day of _August_ one thousand eight hundred and _Sixty Two_ to serve _Three_ years or during the war, is hereby **Discharged** from the service of the United States this _Eleventh_ day of _June_ _1865_, at near _Washington D.C._ by reason of _General Order War Dept May 18 1865_ _regarding to the discharge of men whose term of service expires prior to Oct 1st 1865._ _No objection to his being re-enlisted is known to exist._

said Christian S. Reed was born in _Chester County_ in the State of _Pennsylvania_ is _Twenty Two_ years of age, _Five_ feet _9½_ inches high, _Fair_ complexion, _Grey_ eyes, _Black_ hair, and by occupation, when enrolled, a _Farmer_.

Given at _near Washington D.C_ this _Eleventh_ day of _June_ _1865_.

Jacob Clark
Capt 16th U.S. Infantry
A C M P O Dep 14th A.C.

A.G. Murphy Capt
Co K 92 Regt O.V.

33

1. Williams, <u>History of Washington County, Ohio</u>, H. Z. Williams and Brothers Publishers, 1881, pp. 655-660.

2. Notes compiled by Miss Eliza Brooks.

3. Jerry Devol, Postal History of Lawrence Township, 1967

4. Ibid

5. Ibid

6. Ibid

7. Ibid

8. Ibid

9. Ibid

10. Ibid

11. Ibid

12. Ibid

13. Ibid

14. Interview with Mrs. June Hendershot, November 18, 1975.

15. Interview with Senior Citizens, March 11, 1976.

16. Ibid

17. Ibid

18. Interview with Elmer Miller, February 23, 1976.

19. Interview with Reed Hanna and Walter Hoff, February, 1976.

20. Williams, <u>op. cit.</u>, p. 664.

21. Interview with Dean Becker, August 21, 1975.

22. C. B. Allman, <u>Lewis Wetzell</u>, pp. 106-108.

23. Hanna, <u>op. cit.</u>

24. Williams, <u>op. cit.</u>, pp. 663

EDUCATION

The forefathers of our country provided for education in the
"West" even before the land was settled. The Ordinance of 1785
provided for surveying and selling of land in the Northwest
Territory. Land was divided into six mile square townships with
each township having 36 mile sections. It further provided
that section 16 or 1/36 of every township would be reserved
from sale for maintenance of public schools. The Northwest Ordinance of 1787 further declared "schools and the means
of education shall forever be encouraged." The first schools in
Ohio were maintained by private subscription or rate bills. Thus
it was only open to those who could afford it. Many early settlers
were slow to accept the idea of free public education. They felt
they shouldn't have to pay for the education of their neighbor's
children. In addition, many felt education would be of little
importance in rural areas. It wasn't until the School Law of
1825 that the first big step was made in setting up a system of
public schools. Property would be taxed at the rate of one-half
mill (1/20 of a cent) for each dollar. Thus, free schools had
been set up for Ohio. Later, in 1849, the Akron Law made Ohio
schools uniform by setting up a system of grading and putting schools
in charge of a Board of Directors. The board would establish primary
schools, make and enforce rules, employ and pay teachers. The state

government had taken upon itself the important responsibility for Ohio's free school system.

So with this as background we will now proceed to tell the story of education in Lawrence. "The first school in the township was opened about 1810, by a young man from Virginia, named Dunkin, in a log building which stood on the Joseph Caywood farm, a short distance below the mouth of Cow Run. A schoolhouse was afterwards built on the farm owned by John Templeton, in which school was maintained until the common school system went into effect. A school was opened about 1835 on the J. H. Dye farm, by Peggy Hill. (Miss Hill is buried in Dye Cemetery.) The school was quite popular among the settlers and was well patronized. The only other private school in the township was on Fifteen Creek.

"In 1838 when the public school system went into effect, the township was divided into eight districts, and a log house built in each. The number of districts was increased to ten, and in 1880 to 14."[1]

The first schools were very rude log structures, usually with dirt floors and the inside walls packed with clay mortar. The furniture consisted of rows of benches and a fireplace to heat the school. Reading, spelling, writing, and arithmetic were the main subjects. The early schools had no system of graduation.

By 1938 there were no one-room schools in Lawrence Township, but the Little Muskingum rural district still maintained three one-room schools in adjoining townships. The upper six grades went to Lawrence High School in Dart.

Perhaps Bill DePuy's description of the one-room school is the most accurate. Mr. DePuy, who is one of the oldest citizens in the community, served on the Board of Education in Lawrence for 18 years. He spent most of his life working oil wells in the area. While talking to him, he recited this poem from memory.

> I remember when I went to school
> Some of us walked, some rode a mile;
> To a one room house upon a hill
> Went Mary, and I, Fred and Bill.
>
> Our teacher had forty scholars
> Her monthly wage was sixty dollars;
> She taught eight grades from nine to four
> And banked the fires and swept the floor.
>
> Her subjects were not just two or three
> She taught them all from A to Z;
> She taught us how to spell
> In that one room school we loved so well.
>
> Seated two in a seat, our faces red
> We tried to grasp what the teacher said;
> Our lunch was a homemade sandwich or two
> We had no cafeteria to serve hot stew.
>
> We needed no gym to make us strong
> That two mile walk was plenty long;
> I am told kids are learning more today
> From specialized teachers with higher pay.
> But I remember that one room school
> Where we all were taught the golden rule.

Bill who just celebrated his 93rd birthday, said he doesn't know what book the poem comes from, but he had it memorized perfectly.[2]

Lawrence Township was very fortunate in regard to educational funds in the 1870's. In 1869, when the "oil boom" hit Cow Run, a company named the School-house Company leased from the school board a lot where the Cow Run school stood. The company received two-thirds of all oil yielded. As luck would have the "school house well" became a great producer of oil, and the school board was paid for the other third. The well produced 50 to 60 barrels a day at first, then later increased production to 1,600 barrels a week. The school district received in excess of $40,000 over the years the well produced. There was a great debate over what to do with the excess money. New township schools were built and old ones maintained. Many people favored the building of a college in the township. Unfortunately, the well was not able to sustain itself forever."[3]

One of the people we interviewed who helped us considerably in filling in the links of education in the township was Dean Becker. Ruth Cline, Mark Binegar, and myself talked several hours to Dean one night. Dean, along with his wife, Thalia, taught school for a combined total of 84 years. Dean spent most of his 46 years teaching in Lawrence Township and Thalia spent all but two of her 38 years, teaching in Lawrence. Dean went his first two years of high school at the Upper Moss Run High School, the first high school in the township. It was established in 1921 as a two year high school. The first teacher at the Upper Moss Run High School was Charles Weinstock. There were approximately 12 students in that first high school. Among them were Dean Becker, Senior Lenington, Wilbur Hoff, Fannie Hamilton, Lois Hamilton, Mildred Hendershot, Lora Whitney, and Carroll Pfeiffer. Dean told us Carroll Pfeiffer was one of the most respected and admired students. It was said Carroll never saw daylight at home. He left for school very early at dark and it was dark by the time he returned, as he came the farthest distance. It seems he was also an excellent and dedicated student. Elmer Miller told us that today Carroll is a college professor. These early students either rode horseback or walked to school. Some stayed at boarding houses during the school week. The Upper Moss Run High was a third grade high school and lasted only two years, until 1923. That first high school had one room and was located near George Reed's place. Today, the George Reed place is where Bob Westbrook lives. In 1923, two rooms were rented from George Reed in his house. Now, they used two buildings. They put a telephone line between the two school buildings. There were now two teachers and students had five minutes to change classes from building to building. Science and math were taught in the upper building and English, spelling and history in the other. Two other high school teachers who taught here in the beginning were Paul Henning who came in 1922 and Morgan Ruffener in 1923. Dean particularly remembers Ruffener. It seems

they were squirrel hunting one morning, when Mr. Ruffener slipped

"Lawrence Township High School"

and fell with his gun loaded. The gun went off and Dean got a

14 shot in his leg.[4]

Finally, in 1925 a new, four-year high school was built

and was named the Lawrence Township High School. Some of the

first teachers here were A. H. Vernon, Helen Pickrel, and

Crystal Simms. The first graduating class had 13 students. In

addition to those students listed as starting 1921, were

W. H. Web, Howard Noland, Ada Wallenfelz, Helen Heldman, and
Leslie Brooks. Their graduating picture can still be seen
at Lawrence Elementary School. This new high school that was
built in 1925 was located where Bob Kidd lives today.

In addition to this new high school there were still many
one-room schools for grades one through eight in the township.
We have tried in our research to uncover all of these.
One of the one room schools was Sitka, located at the mouth
of Cow Run where Mildred LaFaber lives today. Some of the
teachers here were Tom Farson, John Gearhart, and Clarence
Weinstock. These teachers were at the school at different
times from approximately 1900 until 1918. One subject that was
different from today was orthography. This is the study of
words by looking at vowels and consonants in pronunciation.
They wrote on paper tablets and slates. There was a water
cooler made of crockery where all students drank from one cup.
Some of the other one room schools, over the years, were Upper
Cow Run, Lower Cow Run, Clark School, located where the
Lawrence School's ballfield is today, Upper Moss Run, Lower
Moss Run, Upper Eight Mi [27], Lower Eight Mile, Hune, Bear Run,
Smith, Oliver, Schramm, and Fifteen School.

"This was once Moss Run grade school"

We will now provide our readers with as many facts as we could uncover about the various one room schools. John L. Hall was the teacher at Fifteen School for some years. He even wrote a book entitled City Tales For Country Boys. He was known for his fairness and strictness. Laura Miller taught at Sitka, Moss Run, and Cow Run. Schramm School was located on Pleasant Ridge near Baird Oliver's home. Oliver School was also located on Pleasant Ridge, named so after the many Olivers who settled on Pleasant Ridge. Some of the teachers at Schramm School were Sophia Romire, Edith Oliver, Edith Pepper, Chester Dye, Fanny Smith, and Pearl Watchler.[5] Smith School was located on a level spot over the hill from the Smith Farm, now occupied by Arthur Smith and family. In winter the only means of

42

transportation to Smith School was on foot or by horseback, and at times the mud was almost impossible. Some of the teachers here were John Lee Hall and Ethel Henry, who retired from Lawrence Elementary in 1974. Some of the teachers here before 1916 were Gilbert Henning, Bessie Gorby, Ceola Patterson, Harry Conner, and Lawrence Dye. Arthur Henning, Harold Hill, Laura Miller, Garnett Busche, and Rev. Lafayette Cline taught here after 1916. Dave Hendershot taught at Moss Run for many years.

Students in these earlier days were responsible for their own transportation to school. Later, school buses were purchased by individuals to transport students. Elmer Miller and Lawrence Smith both owned school buses for many years. Finally, the Board began purchasing buses and hiring drivers.

It seems incredible to us today that one teacher could teach all eight grades. Early teachers not only did this, but they did an excellent job. Some argue that indeed more learning took place then. That, it seems, is an academic question. These teachers, however, must have been very dedicated. They certainly had almost no equipment and their salary was very low. In fact, during the depression some teachers didn't receive any salary for some time.

From the experience told us, school in the one room schools was hard work but mixed with fun. Spelling bees were very popular, with different schools sometimes competing. Students looked forward,

as they do today, to Thanksgiving and Christmas programs. Games

"Dave Hendershot with his class at Moss Run School."
1905

"Bear Run School"

such as hide and seek, dare, red rover, upset the fruit basket, and

others were played. Many of the teachers played fox and hound

with the kids. Box socials and pie socials were a means of raising

money needed for extra supplies. People from miles around attended

these gatherings.

According to Mr. Becker's account, basketball was first

introduced in 1924 in the high school. They had to play Lowell,

the county champs that year. Lawrence had never played on

a floor, before, and some students had never seen a formal basketball

game. Lawrence lost 45-7. Dean said Elmer Miller was a fine

shot. What a tradition was started! Since then Lawrence

45

High School has produced many fine athletes and won the county tournaments several times.

It is interesting to note that all the people we talked to seemed to remember most their education years. This indicates the huge impression our early education makes on our lives. Lawrence can be very proud and fortunate for the many fine and devoted teachers they have had.

The beginning of the end came for one room schools in 1929. A new era was started.

In 1929 the first consolidation took place in which Lawrence Township united with parts of Liberty and Independence Townships. The consolidation was mandated by the State Department of Education. From the September 2, 1929, Board of Education minutes comes this resolution; "whereas the County Board of Education having created a new school district consisting of Lawrence, southeastern portion of Liberty, and all of Independence with the exception of the southeastern part to be known hereafter as Little Muskingum Rural."

"And whereas the following men William DePuy, William Bohlen, Everett Edwards, William Heldman and Arthur Henning were appointed as members of the new Board." The letter included shows the necessary requirements Independence School District had to fulfill.

Lawrence and Liberty received similar letters, but they were unavailable. Thus, September 3, 1929, marked the consolidation of the three townships into one school district. At that organizational meeting of the Board, Bill DePuy was elected the first president and Everett Edwards, the first vice president of the School Board. Since these first board members were appointed, the first election was held that November for board members. That November of 1929 there were four candidates for a four-year term, three to be elected. The candidates were H. B. Clift, William DePuy, William Bohlen, and Arthur Henning. There were three candidates running for a two-year term. They were Martha Schmeltzenbach, Everett Edwards, and Ernest Hamilton. The reason for the terms being two and four years long was for future elections. There would always be at least two board members not up for re-election, thus keeping experienced members on the Board at all times. The winners of that first election were Bill DePuy, Bill Bohlen, Arthur Henning, Everett Edwards and Ernest Hamilton. Also a bond levy was passed that fall as required by state recommendations. The grand total of funds appropriated for 1930 was $37,254.27. That is a far cry from what the annual appropriations are today. At the June 2, 1930, meeting the Board employed the following members:

Ida Hoskin—Superintendent at High School
Christina Stage—Teacher at High School
Laura Miller—Sitka School
Jessie Becker—Moss Run School
Lois Hamilton—Bear Run School
Fannie Hamilton —Centennial School
Glen Duvall—Eddy School
Jessie McGregor—Clark School
Dean Becker—Schramm School
Gladys Malone—Patterson School
J. L. Hall—Fifteen School
Ethel Decker—Smith School
Glen Biehl—Knob School
Beryl VanFossen—Archer's Fork School[6]

In 1930 there were 12 one-room schools in the new

district, seven of which were in Lawrence Township, along with

the high School. These schools were heated by coal. Throughout

the next 40 years, the district had to pass several operating

levies. Every levy ever brought up to the people was passed.

This points out the concern the people of Lawrence have for the

education of their children. Probably one of the most important

things the Little Muskingum District did was the erection of the

Lawrence High School. Today, that building is Lawrence

Elementary School. At the September 26, 1934, meeting it was

moved by Arthur Henning and seconded by Bill DePuy to grant

the erection of the new high school to John E. Mahnken of

Marietta for $21,279.43. We have reprinted that original contract

from Board records. The new high school was first occupied

by students in the Fall of 1935. During the depression years,

manual jobs were given to needy people for high school improvement work. It was funded through one of Franklin Roosevelt's federal

assistance fund projects.[7] In 1938, a new gymnasium was added

to the high school. Many people have watched many fine Lawrence

teams coached by David Hoff, now a teacher at Waterford, and

John Lazear, now a counselor at Frontier High School. In 1944-45

there was even a woman varsity basketball coach by the name of

Betsy Augenstein, who now lives in Marietta. She told me

she was the first woman varsity coach in Ohio. Her team had

a fine season that year, placing second in the county tournament.

She drove the team in her 1940 Ford to away games, having to

use tractor gas due to rationing.

     Gradually, all the students going to the one-room grade schools

were absorbed into the building at Dart. The schools were then

sold by the Board. Most of these original schools are not

standing today. By 1942 all the students in the district were

attending the high school building. The graduating class of 1958

planted the trees that now stand along Route 26 in front of the

school. It is important to mention Ida B. Hoskin, who served as

teacher and administrative head of Lawrence High School for over

30 years. Perhaps the description of the Senior Class of 1960

said it best. They dedicated their yearbook, "The Eagle" to

Mrs. Hoskin. These words are taken from that yearbook, "This

edition of the Eagle is respectfully dedicated to Mrs. Ida B.

Hoskin, our Executive Head.

Ida B. Hoskin, Superintendent

"Mrs. Hoskin has been of signal service to Lawrence High School. Through her determination and hard work we were able to build a gymnasium and enlarge our building several years ago. She is fair in all her dealing with the student body. We, the Seniors of 1960, are glad to take our place with the many alumni who admire and respect this gracious lady.

"We wish her happiness in the years ahead and may (she remember her)——a trusted friend and a wonderful person."

From the many people who worked with and knew Mrs. Hoskin, came many stories of her endless work to make Lawrence a better school. She spent many nights in the school she loved. Mrs. Hoskin passed away in 1975.

The Board of Education minutes researched came to an end in 1964. That year marked the end of the Little Muskingum School District. Lawrence consolidated with Newport, New Matamoras and Bloomfield. We are still in the midst of that new era. Lawrence Smith, who was the clerk for our school district for many years,

"Frontier High School"

Lawrence Elementary

became the clerk for the new school consolidation named Frontier Local School District. For the next four years students continued to go to their respective high schools until the Fall of 1968, when the Frontier High School building was completed. That year, students in grades nine through 12, began attending the new school for the first time. The first superintendent of Frontier District was Richard Hayes. The respective high schools became grade schools with the exception of Bloomfield. Today, Lawrence has grades Kindergarten through eight, having 240 students. The principal is William Zartman, and the present Board of Education is Mary Carson, Lowell King, Raymond Hoff, Edward Rinard, and Delbert Mason. Mr. King represents Lawrence District. The present superintendent is Bruce Bridgeman, who will be replaced by Charles Brown, as Mr. Bridgeman has resigned at this writing.

I have elected not to list the many teachers, administrators, secretaries, cooks, bus drivers, and any other who, over the many years, have made Lawrence an outstanding educational facility.

First row: Cecil Biehl, Gale Heldman, Carl Miller, Howard Hall, Richard Hoff

Second row: Dick Biehl, Leonard Starkey, Wilmer McKibben, Delbert Westbrook, Orin Eddy, Howard Steinhoff, Elmer Taylor, Betsy Augenstein

"MISS BETSY with her fighting EAGLES"

The Board of Education met in regular session with the following members present:

this being the day that was set for the opening of the bids for the
school building.

The following were present:

It was moved by _Arthur Henning_ and seconded by _W. E. Veley_
that the General _____

be awarded to _John E. Anderson_, at _his _____ of
$21,279.43_, with the addition of alternate bid No. _6, 7 & 9_

and the addition of alternate bid No.   #

total of _$21,426.38_, subject to the allowance of the
~~Removes~~ _State Department of Education_

I, Willie Boehm, Clerk of the Board of Education of the Her-
kingun Rural School District, Hamilton County, Iowa, _____ that
the funds necessary to pay the above obligation _____
are not appropriated to any other purpose.

Willie Boehm
3-6-57

Roll call:

Arthur Henning, Herringshofer, W. E. Veley
Dr. Boehler, aye.

It was moved by _Arthur Henning_ and seconded by _Wm. Veley_

RECORD OF PROCEEDINGS

STATE OF OHIO
DEPARTMENT OF EDUCATION

July 9, 1929.

To Board of Education
Independence Rural School District
Washington County

H. B. 510 passed by the last General Assembly and signed by the
Governor authorized $1,000,000 for each of the next two years
for rehabilitation in the state aid districts. A careful survey
of your district indicates that you need the following improvements:

A 4 room brick elementary building to immediately provide for
Patterson Hall, Archers Fork, Knob, Eddy and Centennial schools, and
such other schools as can be later brought to this center. The
elimination of these schools will reduce the number of teachers needed
by 2, thereby effecting a net saving of from $1000 to $1500 per year.

Estimated cost - $18000 to $20000 including site and equipment.
The amount and conditions under which your district can praticipate
in this appropriation are as follows:

That this district receive $2500 in 1929 and $2500 in 1930 from the
state rehabilitation fund to be applied on acquiring a site, erecting
and equipping the four room brick building outlined above under the
following conditions:

1. That the district at the November 1929 election vote bonds necessary
to provide additional funds to acquire a site, erect and equip this
building for school purposes.

2. That when this building is completed the five one room schools listed
above be abandoned, the buildings immediately sold and the funds
obtained therefrom applied on this construction.

3. That the location, plans and equipment be approved by the State
Department of Education.

Action must be taken by the Board accepting or rejecting this
proposal within ten days of the date mailed from this office, and one
copy returned to the State Department of Education at once.

J. L. Clifton
Director of Education.

Approved _____

Board of Control _____

per _____

1. Williams History of Washington County, Ohio, H. Z. Williams and Brothers Publishers, 1881 pp. 660.

2. Interview with Bill DePuy, July, 1975.

3. Williams, op.cit., p. 660.

4. Interview with Dean Becker, August 21, 1975.

5. Interview with Baird Oliver, March 11, 1976.

6. Little Muskingum Board of Education, minutes.

7. Ibid

This is the present Lawrence Town Hall.

This is the township garage.

The stronghold of America has been ingrained in its tradition of democracy—the will of the people being carried out through elected representatives. In one relatively simple document, namely The Constitution of the United States of America, the "founding fathers" laid down the foundations of our democratic government which has lasted since our country's beginnings.

Any society, regardless of size, must, to accommodate itself, have some system of ruling or government. We are fortunate to live in a society whose system of ruling is democratic. So, with The Constitution, the precedent was set for establishing state and local governments as being democratic.

With this as background, we will now proceed to tell about the early organization of Lawrence Township and its government.

A petition was laid before the commissioners at their June session, 1815. It was signed by Nathaniel Mitchell, John Mitchell, Elisha Rose, John Sharp, and others praying that a new township may be laid out and set off from the township of Newport. It was resolved by the Board that the whole of the original surveyed township number three, range seven, together with sections 17, 18, 22, 23, 24, 28, 29, 30, 32, 34, 35, and 36 in the second township, range seven, be and hereby is established into an incorporated town, to be called and denominated Lawrence, and the inhabitants within said district are entitled to all the imminities and privileges of incorporated towns within the state. The electors in said town will meet at the house of John Mitchell on the second Saturday of July at ten o'clock a.m. for the purpose of electing township officers. The court of quarter sessions directed that an election for two justices of the peace should be held at the same time and place. The election which was held agreeably to this order resulted in the choice of the following officers:

    Trustees—William Hoff, John Newton, and Elisha Rose
    Clerk— John Sharp
    Constables—James Hoff, Elijah Wilson
    Fence Viewers— Jonathan Dye, James Mitchell
    Treasurer—John Dye
    Supervisors—George Nixon, Nathaniel Mitchell
    Justices of the Peace—Samuel Dye, John Mitchell

The township officers were sworn in by Samuel Dye, Justice of the Peace.

On the first of April, 1816, the electors met at the house of Nathaniel Mitchell to elect township officers. John Dye was chosen chairman and Elisha Rose and John Newton as judges of the election. John Sharp was the clerk at this second election where 18 votes were cast. The following is the list of voters:

    John Sharp   Elisha Rose
    William Hoff   John Dye
    James Hoff   Samuel Dye
    David McKibbon   Henry Chamberlain
    Issac Wilson   John Mitchell
    Nathan David   Issac Hill
    Nathaniel Mitchell   Exekiel Dye
    Jonathan Dye   James Mitchell
    John Newton   Alderman Johnson

Nearly half of this list resided in that part of the township which has since been set back to Newport. James Hoff was elected first "lister of taxable property" and John Mitchell appraiser of houses. The first grand jurors from the township were Nathaniel Amlin and Nathaniel Mitchell. Johnn Dye was the first petit juror.

The election of 1820 and subsequent elections for many years were held in a school house on John Dye's farm near the mouth of Cow Run. In 1827, section thirty-two of township two was annexed to Newport, and at the June session, 1840. Lawrence was reduced to its present limits. A township house was built near the center of the township where elections are now held.[1]

So with these humble beginnings, democratic government began in Lawrence Township.

The functions and size of local government change with changes in population, area governed, communication, trans-portation, and other factors. Over the years, the township government has decreased in its importance, mainly due to modern communication and transportation drawing communities closer. Washington County has absorbed many of the former powers of self-government in Lawrence Township. One can easily see this absorption process by examining former township officers and present county ones.

Township government is a division of the county exercising powers of self-government. They may levy taxes, establish parks and cemeteries.

At this writing the trustees of Lawrence Township are Dick Biehl, Foster Reed, and Bob Bowersock. The clerk is John Thomas, Jr. They serve a four-year term with new elections every two years in order to leave an experienced member on the Board at all times. They meet the first Friday of each month at the Township Hall, located on Route 26, near the center of the township. Any member may call a special session. They may also be impeached by petition. The clerk is the treasurer and record keeper for the township. Their meetings are public. The trustees also serve on the County Health Board. Their equipment consists of one grader, one dump truck, and one tractor with a mover and blade. This equipment is housed in a garage located beside the town hall. The township operates on approximately a $30,000 a year budget. The money is distributed to the township by the county auditor according to valuation of the township. The county's share, which goes to Lawrence Township, comes from gasoline taxes and license plate sales. The major responsibility of the trustees today is road maintenance. There are 47 miles of road in Lawrence which require upkeep by the trustees. In addition to this responsibility, cemeteries without active churches are maintained by the trustees. Among these are Rake's Cemetery.

Names of township officials taken from available records of the past.

Constables:
John Boney 1876
David Martin 1876
James McKitrick 1877
Frank Brookmire 1879
Anson DePuy 1879
Richard Bailes 1892
Richard Reed 1904

Justices of the Peace:
John Schrader 1876
Susan DePuy 1892
O. S. Reed 1894
Frank Fleming 1912
Bud Kidd

Trustees:
Elmer Brooks 1924
B. H. Oliver 1924
W. A. Lenington 1924
Fred King 1928
William Weinstock 1930
John Thomas 1930
John Whitney 1930
John Britton 1930
Harry Masters 1935
J. L. Hall 1935
J. H. Greathouse 1935
Harry Farley 1938
Richard Reed 1938
Harvey Martin 1938
Herman Weinstock 1942
Charles Bowersock 1944
Gerald McGregor 1946
W. B. Robbins 1948
Foster Reed 1950
Harold Zimmer 1950

Clerks:
Ray Biehl 1928
Floyd Reed 1935
Lawrence Smith 1938-72[3]

[1] H. Z. Williams & Brothers, History of Washington County, Ohio, pp. 660.

[2] Lawrence Township Records

[3] Ibid

62

RELIGION

Religion has always been an important aspect of life to
the residents of Lawrence. The church served not only a spiritual
need but also filled a social need. To be in this township,
one can almost feel the awesome presence of God.

"The first church built in Lawrence Township was located in
the neighborhood of the first settlement, on the Little Muskingum,
near the Newport line, principally through the influence of John
Chambers. It was a small log building covered with clapboards and
used by all the settlers in the neighborhood, regardless of
denominational differences. The church, after 1835, was regularly
under the charge of Rev. L. D. Bingham and Addison Kingsbury, of
Marietta, until October, 1844, when Rev. Levi L. Fay became
the regular pastor."[1]

Rev. Fay served as minister to this church until Oct. 3, 1877,
when he retired because of health. Shortly after Rev. Fay became
the minister, a church meeting was held July 11, 1846, for changing
from the Presbyterian denomination to that of a Congregational
order. The names of the original Lawrence Presbyterian Church
members were Hanna Caywood, John Dye, Joseph Caywood, Mary Dye,
Elizabeth Dye, Susan Dye, Sophia Dye, James Caywood, William Hill,
Martha Hill, and Elisha Dye.[2]

Levi Fay, Henry Amlin, Amos Dye, and Ezekiel Dye were elected
trustees of the new organization. John Dye was elected deacon.

During the summer of 1846 the old building was abandoned and a new one built on Moss Run.[3]

The people of the church were very strict. Church records show that charges were brought against members for profanity and Sabbath breaking. Infrequently, these charges could lead to excommunication, but usually the church would restore membership after a full confession of sins.

In April, 1866, it was voted to thoroughly repair the church. It was finally completed and dedicated in May, 1869. Rev. Fay bought a church bell in Pittsburgh for $120. As admission to the church, one had to give evidence of personal piety and belief in confession of faith.[4]

Rev. Fay received his formal training at Marietta Academy. From here he continued his training at Lane Theological Seminary in Cincinnati. One of his teachers here was Dr. Lyman Beecher, father of Harriet Beecher Stowe, author of "Uncle Tom's Cabin." It was Rev. Fay's sister, Katie, who began the first children's home. He donated the land to her. During his tenure, according to Mrs. Edwin Young, 828 Second St., Marietta, who is the grand-daughter of Rev. Fay, there were so many Smiths and Dyes in the congregation that when the minister went riding in the early morning and spotted an approaching rider whom he did not recognize, he would call out, "Good morning, Mr. Smith," and if that didn't get an answer, he'd change it to, "Good morning, Mr. Dye" which was guaranteed to elicit a response."[5]

Rev. Fay served the congregation faithfully for 33 years. He is buried in the cemetery behind the present day church in Moss Run. Rev. Fay was originally from Westboro, Mass. Before taking the pastorship at Moss Run, Rev. Fay preached in many churches in Newport, Ohio and Virginia (what is now West Virginia.)

I was fortunate enough to obtain a copy of Rev. Fay's memoirs from the church. One of the particular institutions of the time that Rev. Fay particularly disagreed with was slavery. It seems he was going to the Virginia side of the river to preach the Gospel in 1843, and from his own words comes this story:

"I almost reached my place of destination on the Virginia side of the river, I met a man on horseback on the public highway, who gave a very sudden and unceremonious salute, who turning his horse to head my onward way, and at the same time whipping his

65

horse with his knees and with flaming eyeballs, full of rage, he exclaimed, "If I had a club I'd strike you, you are the chap who got away with eleven of my 'niggers'." With an unsteadied speech, I began to affirm my innocence. But I soon found he was in no condition to be my willing bearer; so to set myself free from his ponderous fist, as he approached me on the right, and especially as I could not see the consistency of a pitched battle on Saturday and a gospel sermon on Sunday, I almost involuntarily, with my riding stick, struck his horse's nose which sent my antagonist back out of my own way, and then another stroke on my own steed, sent me forward on my own way, at the rate of ten knots an hour, and although he attempted pursuit, he found I outdistanced him two rods to his one."

It turned out that the slave owner had indeed had eleven slaves escape from his large plantation, but he had mistaken Rev. Fay for another person. As an ending to this story, Rev. Fay wrote of the slave owner, "With a portly body, weighing about two hundred-fifty pounds, with full cheeks, bloated with whiskey, his countenance ruddy, accompanied with a fierce eye made him truly the ideal of a genuine slave holder . . .[When most of his slaves had died, run away for freedom, and what remained were cruelly sold to the South. This old man was called to his death-bed.] A Christian friend happened to be at his bed-side just before he expired, and asked asked him concerning his views of the future state of existence. His reply in substance was that his only wish was that he could be buried on his plantation hill where he could keep his eye on his dead niggers in the morning of resurrection and as to his dying, he didn't give a damn about that."

Although this incident didn't occur in Lawrence, this township did have its share of slave catchers. Rev. Fay does give one a good description of the religious atmosphere of the times in Lawrence when he writes, "There were some good souls scattered here and there all over this whole region who could sympathize with evangelical religion and help advance such a cause, but the great majority were for other wise . . . whiskey was the motive power, both for men and boys . . . Accidents were common. Profanity and sabbath breaking were notorious . . . I found slavery and intemperance my most formidable foes. Even as late as the Great Rebellion (Civil War) I along with others helped fight the battle of freedom and equal rights. At this period and especially in Lawrence Township, the people were all living in log cabins, or unfinished frame houses, clearing up small portions of the heavy forests for farming purposes, and as they had but few meetings on the Sabbath, visiting was the order of the day. God's command, "Remember the Sabbath Day to keep it holy," was by most of the people very little regarded . . . There was now great work to be done, to combat irreligon, skepticism, and unconditional salvation which in many parts of this region then prevailed."

Rev. Fay's words give an interesting description of the times in 1843. Indeed, his work was cut out for him. Rev. Fay spent the rest of his life preaching and converting people of Lawrence. Church membership over the years continued to grow. Many ministers served afterwards, following the example set by Rev. Fay.

In 1886 the meeting house was once again repaired. Many remodeling activities have taken place over the years to constantly improve the facility. Most of these improvements have been financed by donations.

Since 1935, the church annually holds a homecoming, the second Sunday in October. In 1957 the Evangelical Reformed and Congregational Churches emerged under a new name, "United Church of Christ." In 1959 Mrs. Maude Sperry left the sum of $5,000 to the church, which was used for improvements. In 1969, a new Christ Educational Building was added. In 1972, the church had "Rev. Amanda Miller Day" to honor Rev. Miller who had served as minister since 1952. In 1972, Rev. Edwin McLeod began his duties as pastor of the church.

"Moss Run United
Church of Christ"

Today, the church has a membership of 129. Sunday School has an enrollment of 100. This July, Mrs. Esther Shook will be completing her 26th year as superintendent of the Sunday School. Behind the church is Moss Run Cemetery which is maintained by the church membership. Over the years, many people have donated to the church. (Mrs. Joretta Wheaton is responsible for compiling this information on the Moss Run Church.)

"The Lawrence Baptist Church was constituted in 1840. A log meeting house was built and the few communicants met every Sunday, although no regular preacher visited the congregation until 1844. (Picture shown on following page). During these four years, while the existence of the organization was hanging between fear and doubt, the courageous labor of Lettie Templeton carried the helpless infant beyond the period of danger. She is entitled to the proud distinction of god-mother of the church."[6] The first minister of the church was Rev. J. D. Riley.

In early years there was very little money to pay pastors and visiting evangelists. Records show that Lawrence Baptist Church sent two members into fulltime ministries. They were Rev. Emmet Smith and Rev. Fred Rake. Rev. Smith found and ministered Fairs Oaks Baptist Church in Zanesville, Ohio, from 1889-1894. Rev. Rake served as pastor for several churches in Indiana. He returned many times to Lawrence to hold revivals.[7]

"Lawrence Baptist Church"

70

Of the many ministers who served this church, Rev. O. R. Hoskinson from Marietta served the longest, (15 years) from 1941 to 1956. Rev. Edwin McLeod soon followed in 1958 and effected many changes. He served as a great inspiration to his congregation. In 1973, Lawrence Smith was elected to the Board of Trustees of the Ohio Baptist Convention, the first member of the church to serve in this capacity.[8]

Today, the pastor is Rev. Sherman Snider from New Concord, Ohio. The church is now part of the Marietta Baptist Parish formed in 1970. The church is located on Route 26 near Dart.

"Lawrence Baptist Church"

As with other churches in the township, many improvements have been made over the years. There is an accompanying cemetery near the church. Today the attendance averages 50-55. (We've elected not to mention all the many fine pastors who served over the years.)[9]

Another active church in the township today is the Bear Run United Methodist Church, located on County Road 25 (Bear Run). From imformation collected by Jane Matheny, it seems the church was probably established around 1873. In that year, two tracts of land were purchased by the church from Solomon and Susannah Efaw. The second tract was purchased from George and Tirzah McCain. Persons from the Methodist Church who signed the deeds were John Rake, John Smith, John Miracle and A. W. Sutton. These were probably the earliest members of the church. Work must have begun immediately on the church as the cornerstone is marked 1873. It is said prior to the completion of this structure, meetings were held in a small tool house nearby. Probably the first two ministers were Rev. A. H. Roach and Rev. William Swaney.[10]

On November 22, 1886, the Methodist Church sold the building to the United Brethren in Christ of the Bloomfield Charge. In 1935 the church was switched to the Newport Circuit. Finally, it was merged with the United Methodist Church.[11]

The church has been flooded twice, the last time was in 1948.

Today, services are regularly held. Mrs. Erma Stalnaker is the superintendent and Rev. Joe Henry of Lynch Methodist Church is the pastor.

"Bear Run United Methodist Church"

Still another active church in the township is Pleasant Hill

United Methodist Church. It is located in the northwestern part

of the township near Pleasant Ridge on County Road 42.

The church originated from a revival held at Schramm schoolhouse.

Their first church was built of logs in 1863, but later torn down.

Pleasant Hill United Methodist Church.

It was originally a Methodist Church. The present day church was built in 1888. The property for the church was purchased from John and Gretchie Kimmick. There is a cemetery near the church on land given by a Christian Schramm, and more recently, Edward Miller.[12]

Leonard Warren and Gladys Schramm were the first couple married in the church, on Nov. 22, 1942, by Joseph Long.[13]

Over the years many improvements have been made in the church. A new basement, stained windows, and a piano have been added. The church still has its original bell and bell tower.

At present, the pastor is Rev. Homie Clark.

The most recent church added to the township is the Dart Gospel Church, an independent, fundamentalist church. Robert Cunningham, formerly of New Matamoras, was the founder of the church in 1958. His wife, Ruth, served as the first pianist.

The first services were held in the home of Lowell and Sylvia King in Dart. Rev. Cunningham, who had been a carpenter, designed the church building and with the help of church members, the new church was erected in 1959. With only two rows of ceiling tile up, a plywood floor, and borrowed seats, the first service in the new church was held Easter Sunday, 1959, with 15 people in attendance.

The church was located on the southern side of Route 26, near the Little Muskingum. Flood waters from the Muskingum proved to be a major problem. At one flooding, water was five feet high in the church and when the water receded, the piano was found lying across the pews. Therefore, in 1967, the decision was made to move the church across Route 26 on higher land donated by Lowell King. A basement was later added. The first deacons of the church were Lowell King, Larry Rouse, and Boyd Rutherford.

Today, the pastor is Rev. Claude Mathieu. Average attendance is 85-90. Construction is underway to add new restrooms, a storage area, and nursery. The property includes a mobile home which serves as a parsonage for the church. The church has a youth group and a Bible club for the children.

Mrs. Marlene Rouse supplied the foregoing information about the church. (Picture on following page.)

The five churches already mentioned are the only active churches in Lawrence. Over the years there have been many other churches, most notably a German Methodist, Lutheran, Disciple, Presbyterian, and Episcopalian.

The first Sunday school in the area, so far as known, was taught by Mr. and Mrs. McElhinney. It was organized in 1833 and classes were taught most frequently at Joseph McElhinney's in Lawrence. Another such school was run by Thomas Hughes in a Presbyterian Church in 1835.[14]

Today, churches in Lawrence provide residents a place to ⊔fill their spiritual needs.

"Dart Gospel Church"

1. Williams, <u>History of Washington County, Ohio</u>
    H. Z. Williams and Bro. Publishers, pp. 661

2. Church Records of Moss Run United Church of Christ

3. Ibid

4. Ibid

5. April 9, 1967, Parkersburg News

6. Williams, op cit. pp. 661

7. Church Records of Lawrence Baptist Church

8. Ibid

9. Ibid

10. Church Records of Bear Run United Methodist Church

11. Ibid

12. Church Records of Pleasant Hill United Methodist Church

13. Ibid

14. Williams, op. cit. pp. 662

Catherine Fay Ewing

SITE OF THE
FIRST CHILDREN'S HOME
SUPPORTED BY TAXATION
FOUNDED BY
CATHERINE FAY EWING
1858

These words are engraved on a small and largely unnoticed
monument located 12 miles east of Marietta. It will be our
purpose to give some meaning to that monument. No monument
can possibly measure the influence she had upon the lives she
touched. In the following pages, it is our hope that not only
the people of Lawrence Township, but people everywhere who care
about those around us who are less fortunate, can learn from
the dedication and love of one woman.

Catherine Fay Ewing was born July 18, 1822, at Westboro, Massachusetts, the seventh child of William Fay, a farmer, and Elizabeth Lankton. In 1835 the family migrated to Marietta Township. The eldest son, Levi Lankton Fay had preceded the family. He was later to become a minister and spend most of his time in Lawrence Township. Miss Fay became a teacher by profession. At the approximate age of 22, Miss Fay left home to go to Oklahoma to teach. Oklahoma was then part of the American Far West. There she taught at a mission school for Choctaw Indians. In this particular assignment an event happened that was to forever change her life and thus all whom she touched. Apparently, a young infant was left homeless and Miss Fay had intentions of keeping the youngster. However, the conditions surrounding her at the time seemingly prohibited this. The infant was removed to the care of an Indian couple. In a drunken spree, the infant was killed. Perhaps this became the triggering force in Miss Fay's life. Certainly from what is to follow, it would seem Miss Fay's desire to help those children less fortunate became more determined. As to whether or not Miss Fay felt some responsibility towards the infant's death can only be implied. From her diary, Miss Fay stated,

> "The distress of mind I suffered over this sad affair (the death of the child) so affected my health that I was obliged to leave work among the Indians, and return home; but the desire and purpose has arisen in my heart to have a home where I might care for such orphaned and homeless children."[1]

It was with this divine conviction that Miss Fay returned to

Marietta in 1854. At once she visited the county infirmary

where she found small children in the most miserable of

circumstances. To the director of the infirmary she made

the following proposition:

1. She should take charge of the children in a home built
   by her for $1.00 per capita a week.

2. They would supply a new suit of clothes when she should
   take them.

3. They were to pay one half the cost of medical attendance,
   and in the case of death the burial expenses.[2]

The directors eventually agreed to this. Her means to carry

out this proposition were indeed meager. She had $200 in

savings from her years of teaching, a legacy of $160, and $150

borrowed from a friend. With this small amount she purchased

12 acres on Moss Run, 12 miles east of Marietta. Since there

was only a small cottage on the farm, she immediately started

construction of a home. On April 1, 1858, she received

her first children--eight boys, and one girl, all under ten

years. We can better appreciate her situation by her own words:

> "The Lord knowing my needs sent me two legacies;
> one from my uncle, and one from my aunt. (in
> all, her monies, saved, inherited and borrowed,
> amounted to $500.) My aim at first was to have
> a home where I could take children and support
> them myself; but one day I went to our
> infirmary, where I found twenty-six children
> of every condition amid older people of the
> vilest and most profane characters. Some
> were creeping on the floor amid the old and
> decrepit, amid the vicious, the insane and
> the wretched. To see these children. . . . .
> polluted by such contact, was more than I
> could bear. I went at once to the trustees
> of the infirmary, and got their consent to
> give me the children at one dollar per week.
> They were to find them one pair of shoes,
> and two suits of clothes; they were to pay
> one-half the doctor's bills and all funeral

79

expenses, and I was to do the rest. I had begun in the fall of 1857 to build a house upon my place; but there was a small frame house of two rooms on the farm when I bought it. In this I established myself, and on the first day of April, 1858, I received nine children sent to me from the infirmary. (Miss Fay's youngest brother, Samuel Edward, recalled: "I took. . . . . them to her little log house out in Moss Run.) They were all under ten years of age, four of them were babies. These children, with my hired girl and the men who were building my house made a family of nineteen."[4]

Throughout the next ten years, Miss Fay was to undergo not a small number of trials and tribulations which she managed to handle with her utmost courage and faith in The Almighty. On May 1, 1858, Miss Fay took those children of the proper age to the district school. Here she was to first encounter the prejudices of her neighbors. Once again we turn to Miss Fay's own words to reconstruct for us the actual encounter and result:

"In my agreement with the trustees, I was to send the children to school. Nothing was specified, how nor where, but my plan was to have them taught at home during the winter, and send them to the district school in the summer. When the term began (on the first of May) I took all the children of proper age, five in number, and went with them to the school house. I found, however, that the trustees of the school had left word that not one of them could remain, as they were paupers (for that neighborhood was composed of old Virginia families, who inherited a full share of their ancestral pride), and could not be in the same school with their children, so I took them home.

I could not give the matter up without another attempt, and though I had been told I had better not take them again, I felt that I must, and committing my way to the Lord I went on. When I came in sight of the school house, I saw the trustees and thirteen men standing about the door. The children were afraid and began

to cry, and my heart almost failed me; but
the Lord gave me strength. . . . As I came
up to them, I said: "Good morning," and was
just passing on, when one of the men spoke
and said: "You can't go." "Gentlemen,"
said I , "is there a law . . . that can keep
the children from school because they are
poor?" "Yes, there is," he answered, "And
you will find it so," "No," said I, "There
is not. If you say so, it is through ignorance
or a wilful lie, or you intend to make me
afraid; but I do not intend to be scared out of
this thing." So, taking two of the children
by the hand, I led the rest right through them
all into the school house, gave the teacher
the children's books, and left them there.
As I went out one of the trustees met me at
the door, went with me through the men, and
then left me to go home alone; thanking
God that He had protected me from harm.

As soon as possible I went into town, and, by
the advice of friends, was made guardian of
all the children large enough to go to school.
The next day I took them to the school house
and there I found the trustees. I showed them
the proof of my guardianship, and told them
to reject the children if they could.
They had not thought of all this, and did not
know what to say. So I left the children
there. About ten o'clock they came home cry-
ing, and said that they had been sent home,
and asked me if I was old "Goody-Poor-House,"
for that is what they called me at the school.

The next week the trustees summoned me to court,
where I was kept for four days from my home
where there was sickness, and no one there but
hired help. One of the children died the third
day after I got back. The court decided in
my favor, and I was allowed to send the children
to school".[4]

As one can see, much of the prejudice towards Miss Fay and her

home was from the fact that her children were being permitted

to associate with the children of Lawrence Township. Much

of this prejudice was alleviated when Miss Fay began a private

school at her home and employed a teacher for such purposes.

At this particular point it might have been much easier for her to have given up. Even her brother, Reverend Levi Fay, begged her to give up the idea of sending the children to school. Miss Fay was to be constantly abused and harassed in her charitable undertaking. However, it was her utmost faith and trust in God that pulled her through these times. We can easily see the indignation of the township people when Miss Fay writes:

> "Our neighbors, many of them, were not friendly,
> and had strange ideas concerning my work.
> They thought there could be no good motive in taking
> the children to keep as I was doing (some thought
> I was crazy), or that I must be making money
> out of "baby farming", and out of them too,
> as they helped pay the taxes--so they tried
> every way they could to injure me. Our gates
> were opened at night and hogs and cattle let
> in upon our garden and fields. Our chickens were
> often killed. Once, when I went away to take one
> of our children to a home, I found when I came
> back that all but eight of our sixty chickens were
> dead."[5]

During this particular time period it was custom to refer to institutions as asylums. This connotation applied to asylum was then as now, a place to be avoided. In fact, Miss Fay's name for her establishment came in a dream. There appeared on the wall in red block letters the words-- "CHILDREN'S HOME." We today can appreciate the word home. It implies not merely providing children with food, clothing, and shelter but adding that immense dimension of love. It was with this Miss Fay conducted her home. It is with Miss Fay's diary that we can best be provided with her daily activities:

> "July 1, 1858--Today is just three months
> since the children come. It seems almost
> a miracle to me when I look back and see
> how we have been provided for. The ladies

did well in helping me furnish my house,
only I felt at times out of patience when
I went for some old chair or some other things
with a hired team and often they were
dressed for going out or had company and
would tell me I might have them, but they
would be glad if I would call some other time.
They little thought how precious my time was, and
how little money I had to spend to hire teams.
They little thought of my cares at home, and
my sick baby. Poor Frank, we fear he has consumption
his Mother died with it when he was left at the
poor house. He has never been well. He is one of the
dearest children. No wicked word comes out of
his lips now . . . . .

July 2, (1858):-"I have been to town (Marietta)
today and settled up with the trustees and
bought my first barrel of flour. Mr. (Jasper)
Sprague gave me one before I began and yesterday
we baked the last of it. Only think one barrel
of flour to last a family of eight children,
myself, hired girl, with men all the time--
sometimes as many as eight at work on the house,
to last us three whole months and have enough
is truly wonderful.

August 1, 1858: -"We have got moved at last
in the new house. The men have all left
but one and he has much to do to hang doors,
fix cupboards, etc. Oh, it does
seem good to have room to move about after
being so crowded most four months. I now have 16
children. Little Frank seems ripening for
heaven. The children all love him so much
and he has good influence over them. He won our
love by his patience and gentleness. When I
sing any little song (Some little funny song)
to please the children he will lift up those
beautiful blue eyes to me and say, "Oh no,
Mamma sing, "I want to be an Angel," "or," "There
is a Happy Land, "Do Mamma."

October 2, 1858:-"Today a little incident was
brought to light, the cause of which I
never could account for until today.
When Frank was first taken sick he used
to have vomiting spells every night,
and vomit all over the bed and give me
a great deal of work and trouble. One
night, after being up with him several
times, I had just laid down when I heard
him heave. I got up as soon as I could but
it was too late. Clean sheets, quilts,
night gown and all was to be washed.
I said, half to myself, almost unconscious
of what I really did say (I was ashamed five

minutes after I had said it). "Oh, Frank, you must go without your supper." I remember well his look. I felt the child was not to blame, but I was tired and I felt that the child's supper hurt him. He was only a little ailing then. But never from that day until this week has the dear little fellow touched any supper. No hiring (sic) or tempting morsel or compulsion swayed him from what he felt his duty. Oh, what a lesson here for me. A child only three years old! He told me today all about it. I had a long talk with him and I was happy when with a kiss he forgave me all and may God forgive me, too.

February 6, 1859:-"The cold weather seems to have a bad effect on Frank. All the rest of the children seem to improve in health and looks. There is a life and activity about them that they were strangers to when they came here. (On April 5, 1858, Miss Fay had written:- I have had the children 4 days and every one but the two oldest have been sick. They (Lemuel Grimes, Superintendent of the county infirmary, and his wife, Hannah, Nee Chapman) took off their (the children's) winter clothes to bring them here and (the) change of diet only helped along. One of them had the croup. Oh, such a time! I have so little experience. I fear I shall not do all I can for their comfort. . . .)Mrs. R. (perhaps Mary Robinson) has taken charge of Frank at night. This is a great relief to me. There is something about that child. I can't tell what, that awes even the children. I have often left him in his (high) chair and said to him, "Now Frank, take care of the children until I come back." Most too weak to get around well, he would gently arrange things so that when I came back (he) often had them (the other children) sitting in chairs and all as merry as could be (quietly playing as he had planned). "We is good, ain't we," he would say.

May 10, 1859:-"Today our little Frank passed away from us so calmly. Yesterday he seemed better; wanted to go out and see the chickens, so I wrapped him up, carried him in my arms, all the children following me, much pleased to see Frank out. While there I wearied of holding him so I stood him on a barrel that was there. I found he could not stand. He was as well as usual through the night,

ate as well this morning, but when I took
him up to be dressed he could not hold up
his head. I said to myself aloud, "Poor
boy, almost home. He looked at me so sweetly
and smiled, "In that Happy Land, Mama."
"Oh yes," said I," You are not afraid are you?"
He only shook his head but never spoke again.
He was too weak. He died about noon.
. . . . My first death, my first hope of a
happy entrance into heaven."[6]

One can only guess at the physical and emotional
strain put on Miss Fay in these trying times. During 1860,
Miss Fay and her family were attacked with diphtheria which
lasted for months. Henry Howe talked with Miss Fay years
afterwards. Of the diphtheria, Miss Fay recalled.

"I crawled downstairs and found things in
a dreadful condition." The children gathered
around me so pleased to have me with them
again, and with the help of the two oldest,
a girl of twelve and a boy of thirteen, I
went to work to get things in order, but
soon the sick upstairs needed my attention.
I was too weak to walk; I had to creep on
my hands and knees. There lay six dear
children, very sick, one of whom died the
next day. Thus it went on for weeks.
Many a day I had no one to speak to but the
children. The hardest time came one
evening when I knew that one of the little
ones could not live through the night. I
dreaded to be alone, and just at night I
sent one of the boys to ask a neighbor to
come and stay at least part of the night.
He returned with the answer: "Tell old
Kate she was paid for taking care of the
children, and now she might do it." When
the boy told me this I broke down and cried,
until one of the children came and put his
arm round my neck and said: "God can take
care of us". "So he can', I said; "I will
trust in him." Nor did I trust in vain, for
before dark Dr. Beckwith came, bringing his
wife with him."[7]

It is not to be misunderstood that Miss Fay was unhelped
in her endeavors. Friends in Marietta on separate occasion
raised funds for her home. That there was divine intervention

on her part, there can be little doubt. One incident in particular exemplifies this. Speaking in retrospect to Mr. Howe, Miss Fay relates,

"Wanting some lumber for building purposes a neighbor whom I shall here call Mr. Smith, a man of bad reputation, brought me what he said was 1800 feet. I told him that I would have my carpenters measure it, and, if they found it correct, would take it at his price. He flew into a passion that I should doubt his word in the matter. My carpenters found it some 400 feet short. I took it at that, and gave him my note, payable in three months-- amount $20.30.

"In a little short of three weeks, one Friday it was, Smith came to me and said I must be ready for that note on the next Monday, or he would sue me. I was completely taken aback, and asked to see the note. Then I discovered that he had altered the word "months" to "weeks". I was in great distress. The idea of being sued and thus disgraced before my children and the community was terrible, lone woman as I was. When Smith left I retired to my room, and threw my burden at the feet of Christ. Relief was instant, as it always was. The next morning I answered a knock at the door, and there stood a young gentleman of about thirty years of age in light clothes, and with the blackest eyes I think I ever saw.

"He asked: "Are you Miss Fay, the matron of this institution?" "I am." "Here is a package for you."

"With that he turned on his heel, and before in my astonishment I could even thank him, disappeared.

"Who he was, where he came from, or where he went, I never was able to learn from that day to this, now over twenty years ago. On opening I found it to contain exactly the amount of my note, $20.30."[8]

During the 1860's the United States was ravaged by Civil War. It was at this time Miss Fay had a number of soldiers' orphans in her home. She made many pleas to the county commissioners for the establishment of a Soldiers'

Orphans Home. Partly due to her efforts and many others, a Soldiers' Orphans Home was established in Xenia, Ohio.

During Miss Fay's tenure in Moss Run she had taken care of over 100 children, placeing them in decent homes whenever possible. Yet, somehow Miss Fay managed to exert influence upon legislators to enact a law providing for children's homes all over the State of Ohio. Finally in 1866 Miss Fay saw her hopes realized. An act was passed by the legislature in Columbus providing for the establishment, support, and regulation of 'Children's Homes" in the several counties in Ohio. The bill had been introduced by Mr. Knowles, a representative from Washington County. Washington County immediately made plans to erect a children's home under the new law.

It is important to note at this time Miss Fay had fallen in love with Archibald Ewing, a farmer. He was an assistant to Miss Fay at her home. Finally on August 9, 1866, Miss Fay married Archibald Ewing.

Now that the Ohio Legislature had acted, it became a foregone conclusion that Mrs. Ewing's home would be dissolved and the children removed to the new children's home. From the published report of 1885 from the trustees of the Children's Home, Washinton County, comes this report:

> "At the June session of 1866 following the passage of the act authorizing children's homes, the Board of County Commissioners, Messrs. J. J. Hollister, Dr. James Little and George Benedict initiated proceedings for the selection of suitable premises for the permanent location of the home which resulted in the present site and a contract was made for its purchase. . .Prior to this

> time Miss Catherine Fay had about thirty
> children at her "Home" in Lawrence Township
> under an arrangement made with her by the
> Directors of the County Infirmary who were
> ready to be transferred to the new home as
> soon as the building could be made ready
> for occupation, which occurred the first of
> April, 1867. The first Matron, with many
> of the responsibilities of the Superintendent,
> was Mrs. A. G. Brown.[9]

Thus, the first Children's Home in Ohio, started by the benevolence of Miss Fay dissolved. Mrs. Ewing had been offered the position of matron of the new home but she was told a farmer had already been hired to manage the farm. Thus she replied, "When you leave my husband out, you leave me out also."

Mr. and Mrs. Ewing stayed at Moss Run several years before removing to Marietta. It is not to be misunderstood that Mrs. Ewing stopped trying to change the lots of those less fortunate after she gave up her home. She led an organization for the establishment of a permanent home for the aged. She was president of the Women's Christian Temperance Union in Marietta for several years. Catherine Fay Ewing's final departure came April 4, 1897. The death was simply noted in the Marietta Register:

> Mrs. Ewing's funeral . . . was very largely
> attended, the Presbyterian Church being crowded.
> The front was full of children, each with
> bouquets of flowers, which afterwards
> were thrown into the grave. . .Rev. Solomon
> Fay also spoke--somewhat of personal
> reminiscences and a few words to the
> children that "Aunt Katie was not dead, but
> was in Heaven and wanted every one of
> her children to meet her there."[10]

Today there are many children's homes in Ohio providing for hundreds of children. To say that Miss Fay was directly responsible for this would indeed be an oversight. However, it can easily be argued that through her influence and example, the time with which such action was taken was greatly decreased, for she set in motion an endeavor that could not be overlooked.

Williams, in his <u>History of Washington County</u>, wrote in reference to the first children's home: "The scales of prejudice, however, which gather about the eyes of the public, can only be removed by time."[11]

It has been our attempt to remove this prejudice and tell the story of Catherine Fay Ewing. It is by no means complete. It is the legacy of one woman's love for those less fortunate, less loved, and less cared for. Her influence and example can never be measured. It is with great pride, that we of Lawrence Township, have retold the story of Catherine Fay Ewing.

CATHARINE AMELIA (FAY) EWING AND HUSBAND, ARCHIBALD S. D. EWING

89

Church.   Main Building.

THE FIRST CHILDREN'S HOME, MOSS RUN, OHIO
1858 -- 1867

1 Ralph L. Schroeder, Like Apples of Gold, pp.4.

2 Henry Howe, Historical Collections of Ohio, pp. 882.

3 Schroeder, op. cit. pp. 5.

4 Schroeder, op. cit. pp. 5-6.

5 Schroeder, op. cit. pp. 18.

6 Schroeder, op. cit. pp. 40-41.

7 Howe, op. cit. pp. 824.

8 Ibid,

9 Report of the Trustees of the Children's Home,
   Washington, County, Ohio Aug. 31, 1890, pp.

10 Marietta Register, April 7, 1897.

11 H.Z. Williams & Brothers, Publishers, History of
   Washington County, Ohio, pp. 662.

THE CONTEMPORARY COMMUNITY

The contemporary community of Lawrence, according to 1970 census, consists of 787 people. Since 1900 the population has been slowly declining. Part of this decline can be attributed to the fact many have moved to Marietta to live closer to their jobs.

Most of the adults work in industry at Marietta or nearby surrounding areas. In fact so many area residents are employed at Broughtons and Penningtons, the joke is that without the people of Lawrence there would be no bread and butter. A few still farm fulltime for a living.

Recreation seems to be centered at Lawrence Elementary School, where many such activities are held. The area churches still hold many social functions. As for the youth, baseball teams for the boys and softball teams for the girls have been recently organized. Marietta provides citizens many recreational outlets.

The three general stores in the township provide residents with basic needs. Larger stores in Marietta provide residents with goods and services not found in Lawrence.

Two noteworthy businesses in the township other then the stores, are garages run by the Haught brothers.

One garage is run by Neil Haught at Archer's Fork. Clyde, Neil's father, had moved his shop from Elk Run to the garage at Archer's Fork in 1959.

"Neil Haught's
Garage"

Neil, who had worked for his father, took over the garage in 1965 when his father passed away. At present, Neil does automotive, tractors, and truck maintenance and repair.

The other garage in the township is run by Dean Haught. This garage, located at Sitka, was once the schoolhouse there. Roe LaFaber ran the garage there from 1936 until the time of his death in 1971. In August, 1975, Dean reopened the garage. It is now a general auto repair shop.

"Dean Haught's Garage"

In the fall of 1971, the first Lawrence Parent Teacher

League was formed. It was spearheaded by Gilbert Booth, Bob

Sprout, and Jerry Eddy at the insistance of James Poling,

then principal at Lawrence Elementary. Annually, they hold

many fund raising events. The most productive of these is

the Spring Carnival. Money earned from these events are used to

benefit the school. Playground equipment, gym curtains, water

fountains, cabinets, books, filmstrips, are just a few of the

more notable contributions of the PTL. At this writing, the

president is Jerry Eddy.

"Little Muskingum
Volunteer Fire
Department"

Today, one of the most important organizations in the township is the Little Muskingum Volunteer Fire Department. It not only serves Lawrence, but Ludlow, Independence, and Liberty townships as well.

The creation of the fire department was spearheaded by Arthur Haught, Gerald McGregor, and the late Harry Salzman in 1963. At the time of the creation of the fire department Haught and McGregor were members of the Lawrence Board of Education. Salzman was principal of Lawrence High School. McGregor said that in 1963 there was a need for such an organization. The citizens of Lawrence were simply too far away from fire departments to receive fast, efficient help when needed. Several residents of the community, prior to creation of the department, had incurred severe losses due to fire.[1]

To begin with it was decided by the three men to pass out surveys through the school to residents of the community. The purpose of these surveys was to get the reaction of the residents concerning the development of such a department. Their reaction proved very favorable to such an idea. So on December 17, 1963, the first organizational meeting was held. At that meeting, the first officers were elected and various committees organized. We've reprinted those minutes of the first meeting.

John T. Hall donated the land on which the fire building was to be erected. The land was located beside Dean Eddy's store.

It's important to mention that this organization is almost
totally financed by the community from donations and other fund
raising activities. One of the most important fund raising
events is the fireman's social held each year. It also
receives money from the trustees for fire protection. The
department receives no federal or state financial assistance.

In these early days it was necessary to raise money to
began building the firehouse. In addition to this, equipment
had to be secured, proper licenses obtained, and various other
logistical concerns to be solved. Shortly after the department
was created, the wives of firemen organized an auxiliary. Doris
Congleton was elected the first president. These women raised money
through rummage sales, bake sales, potluck suppers, etc., to
help finance the organization.

In 1964, construction of the firehouse began. With the
exception of plumbing, electrical work, and the laying of
block for the foundation, all work was done by the people of the
community. Many people spent endless hours in these early days
to build the firehouse. To help finance this building, a loan was
made from a Marietta bank. The building was finally completed
July 5, 1965. The new building consisted of a three-bay garage
to house a pumper, tanker, and utility truck. A modern
kitchen was also added to the station.

The fire department began functioning before the new station was complete. They acquired a GD pumper from the Reno Dept. and housed it in Bob Theobald's garage, across from the station being built. Several runs were made from here. A tanker and an old Ford truck were also purchased.[2]

On November 14, 1965, open house was held at the new fire station for the community.

Many significant additions have been made to the fire department. Today, the department has added a new dimension to its original purpose, a $13,000 emergency squad vehicle. Squad members are certified emergency medical technicans. For members to qualify, they must receive 60 hours of EMT training as well as refresher courses every three years. The department does much more than save life and property from fire. They respond to any emergency in which people need help. In 1975, the emergency vehicle made 77 runs. By May of this year, the Squad has made 52 runs. It's impossible to describe the value of this unit to the community.[3]

In talking to people of the community about the department, it becomes apparent that the key to this whole organization is cooperation. The huge success of this operation lies solely in the outstanding cooperation members have among themselves, as well as the community. For example, a call to the LMVFD will ring five phones. The call will be answered by Dean Eddy, Gerald Congleton, Charles Bowersock, Carroll Eddy, and Arthur Haught. Once they know the nature and location of the call, they in turn respond immediately by calling other members. This is the epitome of cooperation.[4]

The department covers one of the largest areas of any such volunteer department. The department also has a mutual agreement with other local departments to respond to their areas when needed. People helped are done so at no charge.

At present there are 43 members. Officers are elected every year. At this writing the officers are:

President—Bob Huntsman
Vice President—Clarence Farley, Sr.
Secretary—Gary Congleton
Treasurer—Earl Westbrook
Fire Chief—Carroll Eddy
1st Ass't Chief—Arthur Haught
2nd Ass't Chief—Gale Depuy
Squad Captain—Juanita Eddy
Operating Engineer—Wayne Eddy
Quartermaster—Gary Hamilton

In addition to the emergency vehicle, there is a pumper, tanker, two portable pumps, Indian tanks (equipment that is carried on one's back) rakes, firebeaters, individual apparrel, portable power plant, and a portapower. At the station is a CB base unit which relays messages from the CB in the emergency squad.[5]

The LMVFD, is a tribute to this community's willingness to help each other.

"LMVFD Emergency Squad"

"LMVFD pumper"

"LMVFD tanker"

"Little Muskingum Grange 2621"

Another important organization in Lawrence is the Little
Muskingum Grange 2621. It is located off Route 26, near Mr.
Robert Kidd's home, on land donated by Mr. and Mrs. William
Bohlen.

The Grange became an important national organization
after the Panic of 1873. The depression drove thousands of
farmers into the Grange in hope of finding some way to improve
their condition. The early Grange in America carried out a
number of activities, all designed to aid the farmer. On a
national level, the Grange provided social contracts for
farm families and showed what farmers could accomplish through
political action.

The Grange in Lawrence was chartered April 27, 1935. The
project was spearheaded by William Bohlen. There were 41
charter members of which five are still active in the Grange.

99

Their early meetings were held in old Lawrence Township High School. During World War II this building was sold so meetings were then held at Lawrence High School in Dart.[6]

In 1957, members began building the present Grange building. This project was financed through a series of projects. The project that generated the most money, according to Bob Kidd, was the growing of cane. Members planted, worked, stripped, and cut the cane. It was then taken to a mill in Stafford where Molasses was made. The new building was finally dedicated in December, 1960.[7]

Along with the Master, the five trustees are the governing body of the Grange. The first Master of the Grange was William Bohlen. Today, the Master is Frank Haught. The present trustees are Wilbur Bohlen, Frank Haught, Ronald Wright, Bob Kidd, and Lawrence Smith. The Grange is designed to serve Lawrence, Independence, and Liberty Townships. Today, the organization is not farm oriented. Rather, its membership

is open to anyone. Today, there are 112 members. The Grange serves an important community role socially as well as carrying out projects to benefit the area. Some of their more notable contributions include giving Lawrence School a piano, donations to special funds, and providing blood pressure clinics for residents. Basically, the Grange serves where it is needed in the community.[8]

The Grange also has a Junior Grange for members under 14.

Minutes of the meeting held December 17, 1963

The meeting at this time of all interested people to organize and elect officers of the Little Muskingum Volunteer Fire Department

The following officers were elected by a ballot vote:

President   Arthur Haught
Vice-president   J. T. Hall
Secretary-Treasurer L. H. Smith

The following persons were appointed to inspect the various sites for the proposed Fire Equipment Building and to report their recommendation at the next meeting:

William DePuy--Chairman
A. H. LaFaber
Robert Rake
Charles Bowersock
Earl Congleton

The following persons were appointed for the Fund Raising Committee:

Gerald Congleton
Robert Sprout
Darrel Haught
Dale Becker
Gerald Kendall
Gerald McGregor

The Meeting was adjourned until January 7, 1964 at 7:30 P.M.

THIS IS A SPECIAL INVITATION TO OUR OPEN HOUSE

The Little Muskingum Volunteer Fire Department and Auxiliary invites you and your family to the open house, Sunday, November 14, 1965, from 2:00 P. M. to 7:00 P. M. at Dart, Ohio on State Route 26. The Auxiliary will be serving lunch from their newly furnished kitchen.

The members and auxiliary of the Little Muskingum Vol. Fire Dept. have worked faith-fully together to build a fire house that shelters the fire fighting equipment that we have, which is used for the sole purpose of saving life and property from fire.

We also want to thank each and everyone who have donated so generously and made it possible for this community to have a Volunteer Fire Department.

In the near future the Members of the Fire Dept. will be visiting every home in our area asking for donations. We certainly will appreciate any donation, no matter how small, you can give.

The following names are members of the Little Muskingum Volunteer Fire Department.

Gerald Congleton—Chief	Edwin Thomas
Arthur Haught	Carroll Eddy
Dean Eddy	Virgil Gearhart
John T. Hall	Raymond Fickesien
Charles Bowersock	Clarence Farley
Robert Bowersock	Willard Ruble
Gary Haught	Bill Becker
Steve Eddy	Gale Becker
Leland Tait	Robert Sprout
Gerald McGregor	James Stalnaker
Gale Bartmess	Jimmy Stalnaker, Jr.
Ralph Binegar	Charles Binegar
Robert Westbrook	Robert Huntsman
Robert Rake	Robert Theobald
Larry Rake	Dick McGregor
George Rake	Wade Becker
David Henthorn	Ernest Wheaton
Frank Haught	Lawrence Smith
Robert Armstrong	Walter Rinard
Richard Hendershot	Thurmond Enoch
Leon Edwards	Merle Binegar
Floyd Depuy	Roe Lafaber

The following names are Auxiliary members of The Little Muskingum Vol. Fire Department.

Mrs. Gerald Congleton	Mrs. Arthur Haught
Mrs. Gale Bartmess	Mrs. Charles Binegar
Mrs. John Hall	Mrs. Willard Ruble
Mrs. James E. Thomas	Mrs. Frank Haught
Mrs. Gerald McGregor	Mrs. Ernest Wheaton
Mrs. David Henthorn	Mrs. Carrol Eddy
Mrs. Robert Rake	Mrs. Thurman Enoch
Mrs. Clarence Farley	Mrs. Robert Theobald
Mrs. James Stalnaker, Sr.	Mrs. Robert Westbrook
Mrs. James Stalnaker, Jr.	

HONORARY MEMBERS

Mrs. George Kalem	Mrs. Mildred Varner	Miss Charolette Thomas

The general characteristic of the township today is cooperation among its residents.

1. Interview with Gerald McGregor, May 8, 1976

2. Ibid

3. Interview with Earl Westbrook, May 8, 1976

4. Ibid

5. Ibid

6. Interview with Robert Kidd, May 7, 1976

7. Ibid

8. Ibid

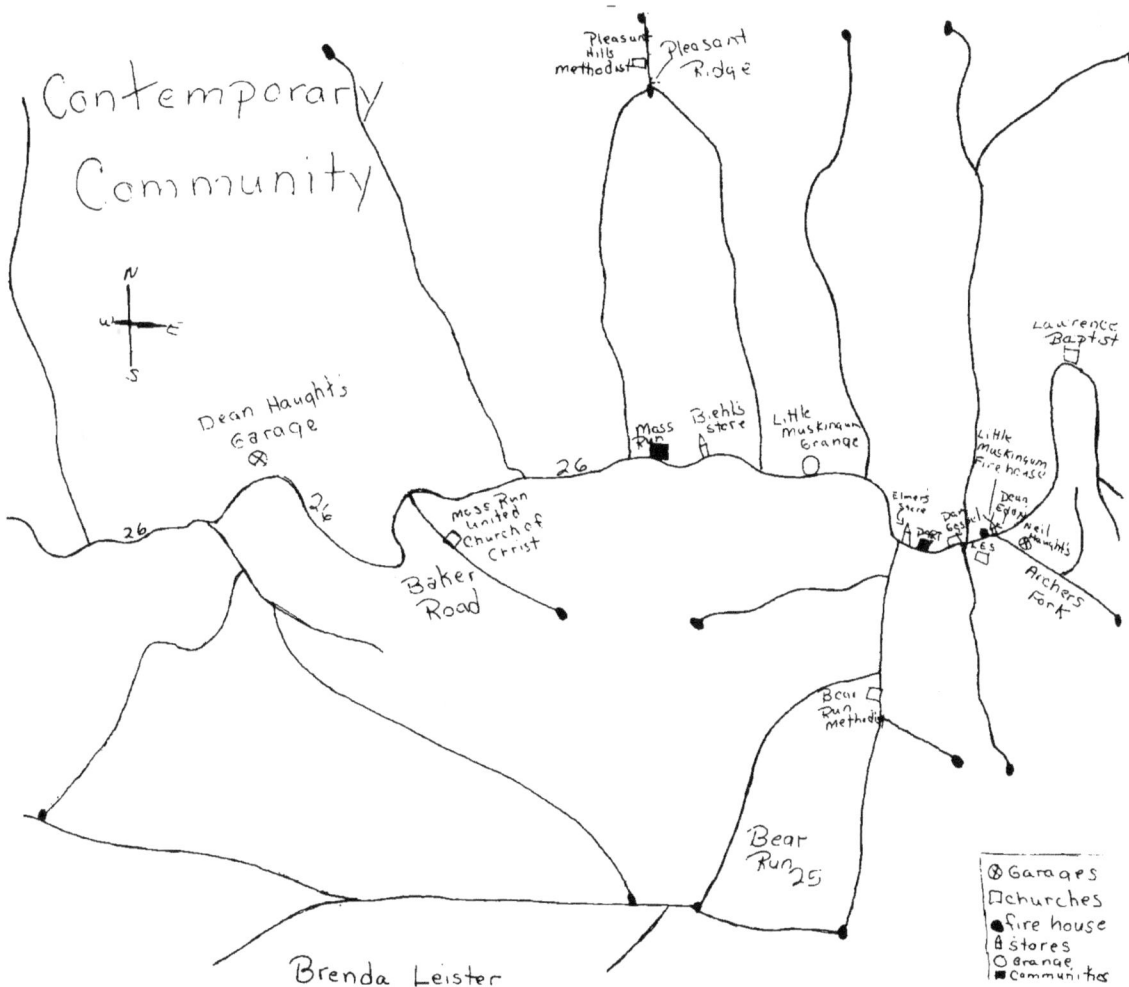

Contemporary Community

Brenda Leister

103

GEOGRAPHY

Basically the many land features have changed little since 1815. The changes that have occurred have been mainly in building roads. More importantly our description and pictures of Lawrence today will serve as a valuable reference in future years. Finally, this section will include a great deal of folklore about how the many roads and geographical features got their names. During our interviews we were told many fascinating stories of name origins.

Lawrence is the only square township in Washington County. It is bounded on the North by Liberty Township, on the East by Independence Township, on the South by Newport Township, and on the West by Fearing Township. No one really knows how the township got its name. However, the most probable theory comes from the War of 1812. James Lawrence was a naval commander under the command of Oliver Hazard Perry. He was mortally wounded during a naval engagement, and his words became immortal, "Don't Give up the Ship!" These words were inscribed on Perry's ship on a banner. Two years later, the township was named in honor of James Lawrence.

The main water body of the township is the Little Muskingum, which enters at the Northeast corner of the township and flows diagonally across the township dividing it into halves.

Other important streams are Bear Run, Cow Run, Elk Run, Moss Run, Baker Run, Hog Run, Fifteen Creek, and Archer's Fork, (which is mainly in Independence Township). There are several saline springs in the township.

Most of the soil in Lawrence is very productive. Thus, much of the land is cultivated and many products grown here. Living off the soil was, until recent times, the main source of livelihood for the people.

Other very important natural resources in the township have been coal, petroleum, and forest land. These have already been described in detail in another chapter.

These, basically, are the general features of the township. The history and economic development of the township were based on these natural resources. One cannot underemphasize the importance of an area's natural resources, for it is within those God given circumstances that an area's history and development takes shape, based on these features. As one reads our history, it should become very clear the role geography played in determining the development of Lawrence.

Without question, the most important road in Lawrence Township is State Route 26. It provides the link to much traveled Marietta. All roads lead to it, so to speak. Route 26 was a dirt road in earlier times, later graveled, and finally asphalted.

State Route 26

One of the roads that connects Route 26 is known as Cow Run in the southern part of the township. The road follows along Cow Run, which flows and empties into the Little Muskingum. "There are saline springs along the entire valley, which before the land was fenced, attracted cattle from the territory from miles around. This was the creek on which the milkmaid was accustomed to find her cows and it is not strange that Cow Run became the common designation.. Cow Run flows through a ravine known as Dark Valley. Here the channel of the stream is very narrow and its course is due north and south. A range of hills on each side rises almost perpendicularly to the altitude of 400 feet above the stream level. From the bottom of the valley, the sun cannot be seen for more than four hours a day."[1]

"Cow Run"

Bear Run is County Road 25 connecting Route 26 with Newport. The run rises in the southeastern part of the township and flows northwesterly. "It derives its name from an event in the life of Archer, the hunter. It is said that on the banks of this stream Archer met a bear in hand-to-paw combat in which the veteran hunter triumphed, not, however, without receiving severe injuries. His thigh was horribly clawed and his life barely saved. Another origin for the name of this stream is that a bear was killed in the valley through which it flows."[2]

"Bear Run"

Fifteen Creek runs along County Road 12 in the central part of the township. It leads to an area in Liberty Township, known as Slabtown.

"Fifteen" (County Road 12)

"Fifteen Creek"

Moss Run is a creek located in the central part of the township. The mouth of the stream is located in the community of Moss Run. There are several theories as to how this name was derived. In earlier times, the area was known as Morse Run. From William's History, it is said Morse Run was named after a man named Morse, who manufactured chestnut shingles. Somehow the name was changed to its present day form--Moss Run. One theory was related by June Hendershot. Lawrence was part of the Underground Railroad during Pre-Civil War days. The underground railroad was a network of homes, hiding places, etc., allowing slaves to escape from the South. It seems Morse Run was a station on the underground railroad and became well known among slaves. However, their southern dialect made them pronounce it "Moss Run". This name stuck. Another theory is that the rocks on the bottom of the stream have moss on them. Whatever the origin the name of the stream and community today is Moss Run.

"Moss Run"

"Moss Run"

At the mouth of Cow Run, is an area known as Sitka. This is
where Route 26 intersects with Cow Run. "Joseph S. Burkey, whose
mother Eliza Hill was of the family that first settled in this
area, while serving with the 22nd U. S. Infantry was drowned from
sailboat, May 12, 1872, at Sitka, Alaska, and thus the Lawrence
township community was named 'Sitka' in his memory."[3]

"Sitka"

Another important community today in the township is that
of Dart. It is located in the eastern central part of the township.
In this community is located Lawrence Elementary School, Neil
Haught's Garage, Dean Eddy's Store, and the Dart Gospel Church.
Dean Eddy told the story of how Dart got its name. It seems in
1905 that William Lennington and Sam Bohlen were trying to decide
what to name the community and its new post office. Suddenly, a
bird came "darting" towards them. That "darting" brought about the
suggested name of Dart, which became both the community and post
office's name. Dean says that the Dart Post Office is the only
one in the country that bears that name.[4]

"Dart"

Steel Run is located in the northeastern part of the township. It was probably named after the Steel family who very early settled the area.

It would be an awesome task for us to try and mention all the roads, hills, ridges, etc., in Lawrence. Therefore we have been selective in mentioning those that are most traveled. No doubt the names of most of these were derived from the people who settled the areas. Some of the roads that run off Route 26 in addition to those already mentioned are Little Eight Mile, Reed Road, Archer' Fork, Clark Hill, and Mosser Road. From these roads are lesser important township roads. Brooks' and Masters' Road run off Cow Run. Cow Run connects Pine Ridge. Binegar Hill runs off Archer's Fork and goes to Eddy's Ridge, which is in Independence Township. Pleasant Ridge extends from Moss Run. Bean Ridge and Davis Hill run off Bear Run. These roads and streams seem less confusing when viewed from our maps. We have included pictures of most of these areas.

Another place needed to be mentioned is "Beckerville," the name given to a section of Route 26. Here, in a small stretch of road, live the children and grandchildren of Allie Becker. Allie is the unofficial mayor. At one time someone even erected a sign on Route 26 designating the area as Beckerville.

"Beckerville"

Once again our purpose in this chapter was to give our reader an idea of the basic features of the township-natural as well as man-made. Hopefully, our folklore of the various places has enhanced this section. No doubt, we have left out some, but not by design.

"Binegar Hill'

"Martin Road"

"McCain Hill"

"Davis Hill"

"Archer's Fork"

"Masters Road"

"Clark Hill"

"Reed Road"

"Neff Ridge"

113

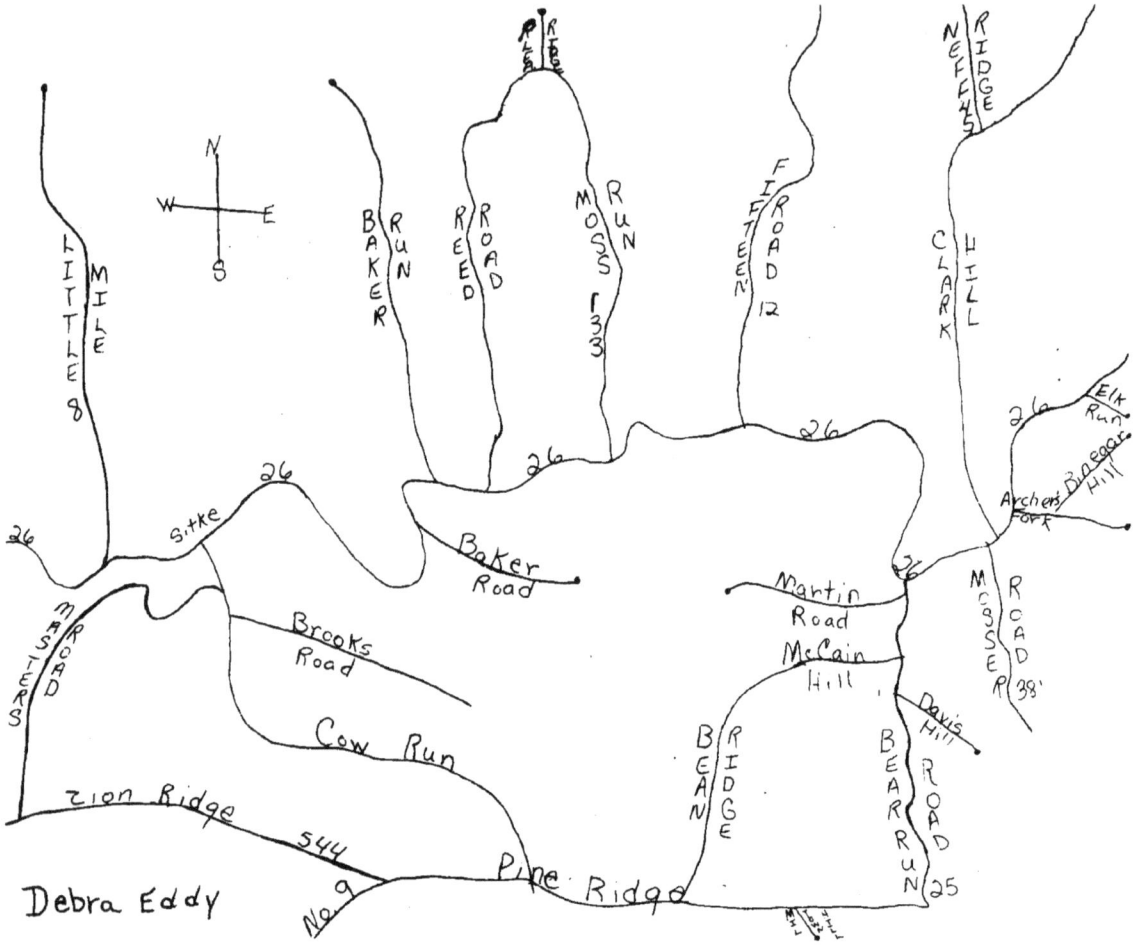

Debra Eddy

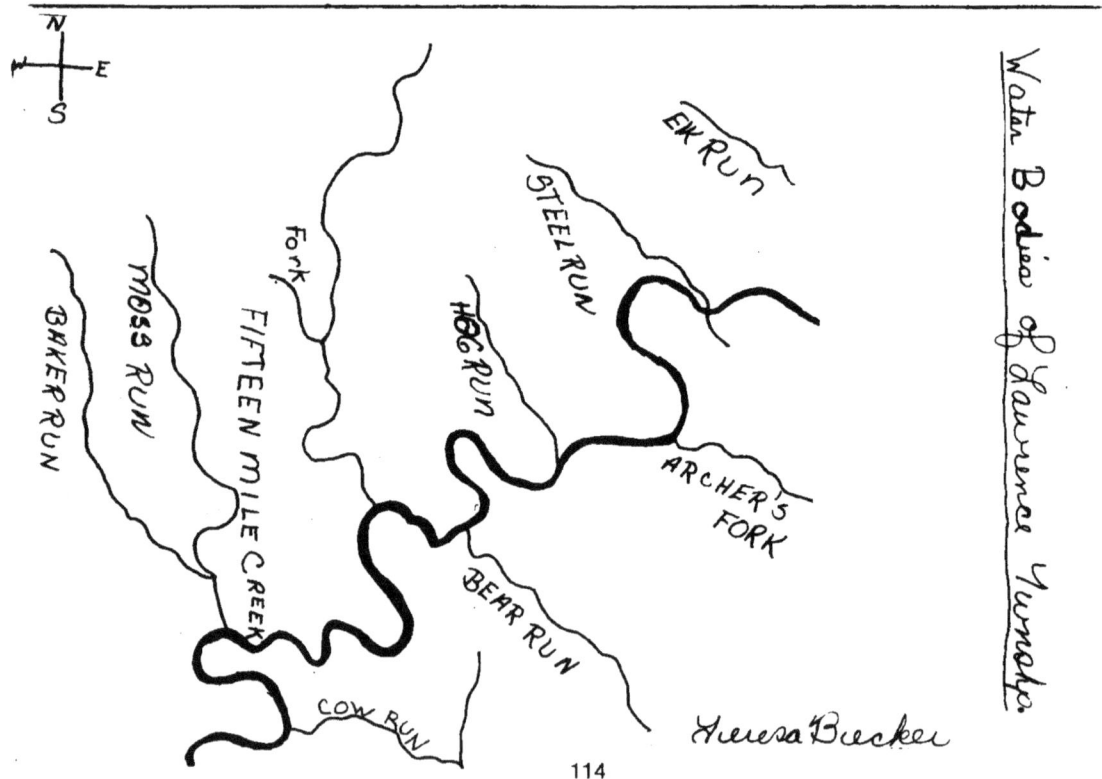

Water Bodies of Lawrence Township

Theresa Becker

114

"Pine Ridge"

"Zion Ridge"

"Little Eight Mile"

115

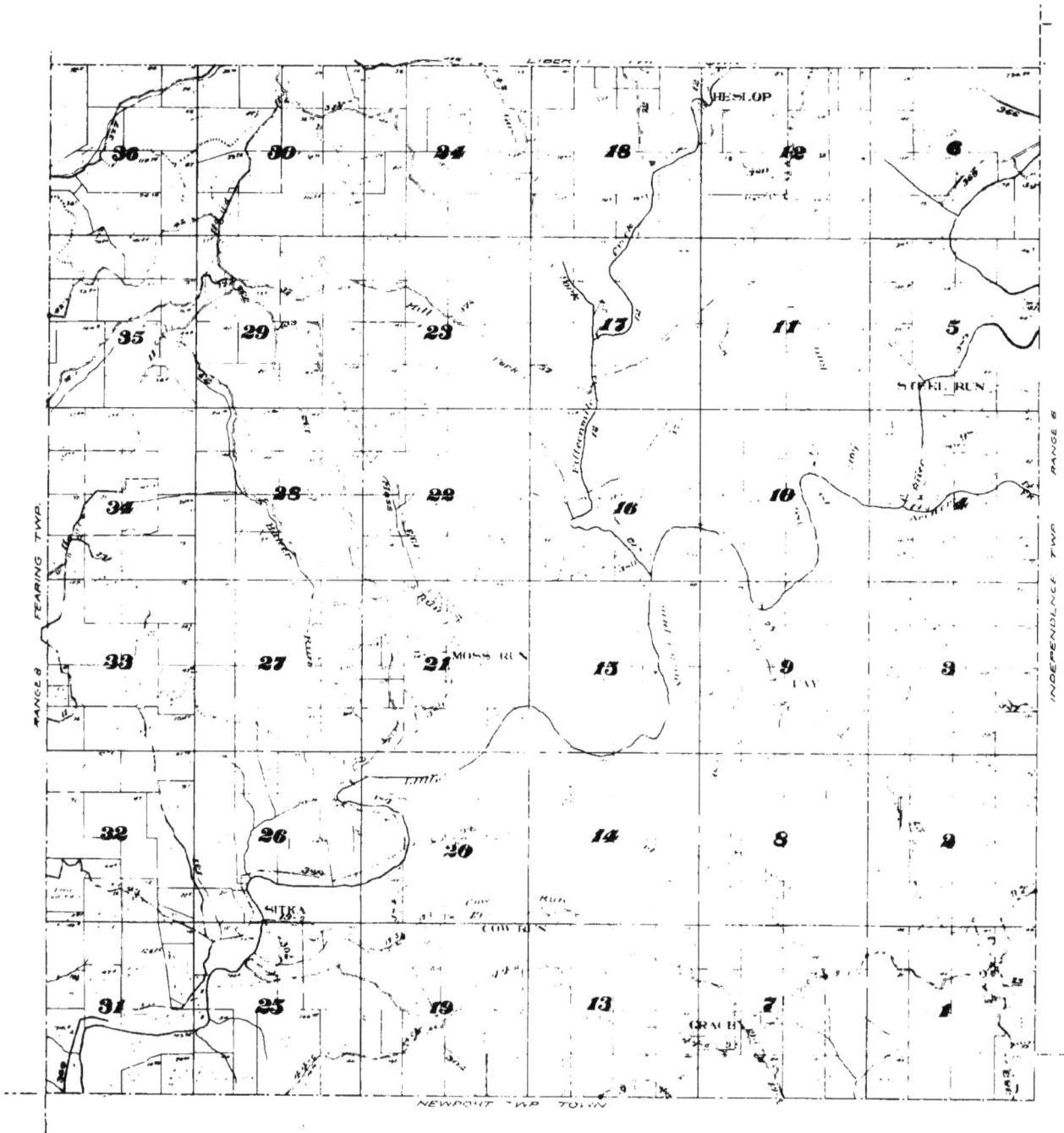

LAWRENCE TWP.
SCALE 4¼ MILE

ECONOMIC DEVELOPMENT

Any society, to survive and sustain its members, must produce or obtain food, clothing, shelter, and other essential items. It will be our purpose in this chapter to discuss the many ways the people of Lawrence have made their living. Indeed, their livelihood, until recent times, has been based on the township's natural resources. It hasn't been until recent times that many citizens have found employment in industries outside the township.

The development of the township's richest resource, oil did not come about until 1860. Up until that time, the early settlers relied almost exclusively upon the land to make a living. These early pioneers managed to bring what livestock they could to include sheep, cows, hogs, and chickens. Most of the township's land was very fertile. Of course, much of this land had to be cleaned of thick forest to allow farming. Corn and wheat have always been important crops, along with oats and hay. At one time tobacco was an important cash crop. Certainly, along with these crops, families, then and now, grow many vegetables for their own use. It's important to mention that much of the township is hilly, and that land was used for grazing, and cattle were raised for commercial purposes in later days. Hogs and poultry also produced much of the farm income.

"Forest land in Lawrence"

As stated earlier, much of the township's land was forest, consisting mainly of poplar, chestnut, hickory, oak, elm, walnut and sycamore. These different types of wood proved invaluable for their many uses. Poplar, because it is light and polishes well, was used to make bedsteads, bowls, wooden dishes and troughs. The elm was used for house building and fuel. The walnut, because of its beauty, was good in making cabinets and furniture. The chestnut was used to make shingles. In addition to these, wood was used to support the mines, to make machinery, build fences, and construct bridges.

Animals were abundant in early Lawrence. There were bears, deer, wolves, wildcats, panther, raccoon, fowl, foxes, and many smaller animals such as squirrels and rabbits. Thus, the early settlers were provided a wonderful source of game. However, it is not to be understood that all these animals were useful. Some, such as the wildcat and panther, were very dangerous. Bears proved an annoyance to the settlers as they carried off hogs and many smaller domesticated animals. From Miss Brooks' account of the township, the last bear ever killed in the township was tracked in the ice of the Little Muskingum to a hollow sycamore tree at the mouth of the Fifteen Creek. It was here that it was killed.

Finally, the Little Muskingum River and its many tributaries provided the settlers with an excellent source of transportation as well as fish for food. Thus, it was from these natural resources that the early settlers made their living.

"Without question, the single most important resource in Lawrence, in terms of money, was oil. William Guyton for 20 years made use of the gas emitting from a fissure on Cow Run to light his shop, and a "burning spring" on Mill Creek had been known since the earliest settlement. But it never occurred to anyone that these phenomena indicated the presence of oil."[1] In fact, in many communities where oil was first discovered it was considered somewhat of a hindrance. The reason oil didn't become an important industry until 1860 was probably due to a lack of scientific knowledge and a desire by most to engage in more substantial pursuits. "John Newton was the first to anticipate the possibilities, and, in partnership with Mophet Dye, began to sink the first shaft, near the summit of the break, on Cow Run. In 1860, oil was found at the depth of 140 feet. It flowed at a rate of thirty barrels a day. The great success of this first attempt greatly aroused the neighborhood. The early operators and pioneers in the business were Newton, Dye, Perkins, Jonathon Hoff, Logan, List, Hervey Ablinas, Green, Brown, and Nailor. The

("Oil Fields in Lawrence")

first engine was brought to Cow Run by Jonathon Hoff. The first

wells were all drilled by spring pole. The first machinery for

drilling was used by George McFarlan in 1864, when the first

attempt was made to strike oil in a lower strata. The success of McFarlan's enterprise gave the business a new impetus. Many of the first sand wells had failed, and the production of others was declining. The discovery of the second sand deposit seemed to insure permanent production. When McFarlan struck oil in the second sand, there was great rejoicing among the holders of the leases. In fact, they carried him about in triumph on their shoulders. Property became food for speculation, and capital was lavishly and recklessly invested."[2] This renewed period was about 1864-1866. It was a time of speculation, drilling accompanied by investors, swindling, prospectors, and drifters. Most of the excitement centered around Cow Run. By the end of 1861 most operations had ceased due to low prices for oil and labor shortages, caused partially by the Civil War. But by 1864 things were in full swing again. In April of 1864 Samuel Dye was offered $35,000.00 for his oil interests. In the summer of 1864, Bergen Oil Company purchased his property along with the interests of James Newton. By July, the market prices rose to $14 a barrel with heavier grades bringing as high as $28 a barrel.[3]

One can only imagine the immediate effects this oil boom had on the township. Cow Run had the appearance of a large camp. Plank houses and tents were spread everywhere. The effects can be seen by the October 13, 1864, edition of the Marietta Register: "Look at our quiet little city! One short year ago, so quiet that strangers always lost their reckoning, and thought when they reached the place, that the day was surely the Sabbath. Now, in some parts of our goodly city, one would hardly recognize the Sabbath at all. Multitudes rushed in their mad haste to be rich.

"Now, the population of our little world is fast becoming
known by the title of oil-men. Merchant princes, the solid
men of this western hub of the union, brokers, bankers, clerks,
and students, college professors and great unlearned are alike
the victims of the oil fever. They talk oil, and eat oil, and
drink oil, and dream oil. Our ministers draw their happiest
illustrations from this unfilling fountain. Says one, "How very
strange it would be to hear of the Apostle Paul turning aside
from the ministry, to speculate in gold, or land, or oil!" . . ."

From an article in Oil News, came this report: "There was a
community of thousands at the Run and the hungry prospector
had a hard time to find rations. I doubt I shall ever see in
this country again such a jam of human beings and capital on
so small a space of territory." As I drove along Cow Run this
spring I stopped and tried to imagine this beautiful, peaceful
place on the site of an "oil boom." A survey made of Cow Run
in 1868 showed production of individual wells:

Willow Well #1	45
Willow Well #2	180
Warren Well	90
De Russey Well	75
Neil Well	55
Baker Well	28
Wilson Well	36

"This production shown was barrels per day. Most of these
wells were owned by the Exchange Oil Company."[4]

Drilling activities really are listless in the 1860's.
The key word was strike! New strikes were constantly being made
keeping the people in a constant state of excitement. The
population of Lawrence in 1860, according to the Atlas of Washington
County was 1,627. By 1870 the population was 2,860. This gave

122

Lawrence the highest population in the county, with the exception of Marietta.

Between Cow Run and the Ohio River, two inch pipe was laid, having capacity of forty barrels per hour. Wagons and teams hauled much of the oil. The Marietta Board of Trade reported for the week ending February 28, 1870, the Cow Run production at about 550 barrels a day. Moss Run and Fifteen had only a few productive wells. "One of the most important wells drilled was owned by Dye, Chamberlain and Turner, and was called the "School House Well." It was located on the school house lot under a lease from the school trustees, to whom a royalty of 1/3 was paid. The school house was moved and operations began which resulted, on the twenty-second of October, in procuring probably the best well in the township. At first it produced 120 barrels a day. In 1869 and 1870 about 500 wells were being operated, and shafts were being sunk wherever a show of success presented itself. Production decreased rapidly from 1872 until 1876."[5]

Today in Lawrence there is still oil production. Wells and rigs serve as only a reminder of the great boom days of the 1860's. The effects of the oil industry were many. Indirect benefits found their way to farmers, merchants, mechanics, and manufacturers. The farmers found a market for their products in the oil fields and trading centers. Teams and wagons made money by hauling oil and equipment. Timber sales were stimulated by the production of wagons and oil barrels. Land values for everyone were enhanced. The population zoomed over these oil years, and the more population an area has, the more goods and services it requires. In all this, many jobs were created. For the most part, Lawrence citizens were now engaging in (the livelihood) other than farming. Indeed,

123

the oil boom was one of the most exciting chapters in the history of Lawrence.

Farming has always been an important aspect of the citizens of Lawrence. Certainly, many changes have occurred over the years to make it more scientific and modernized. However, we hoped to talk to someone who knew how it "used to be done." Baird Oliver was that someone. He related what typical farmlife was like in in the early 1900's. Wheat, he said, used to be cut with a hand scythe. Later, they used a wheat cradle and binder, powered by horses. The wheat was then stacked with twelve sheaths in a stack. Ten bundles were set up with two around it. The wheat then set until it was good and dry before hauling it to the barn in a wagon. Once in the barn, a thresher powered by a steam engine was used to separate the wheat from the straw. After threshing, the wheat was then stored in a granary. From here, there were several uses. Some of it might be taken to the mill to be ground into flour. Middlings were fed to the cattle. Finally, some of it might be sold outright.

Hay was planted just like wheat. It was cut with a mowing machine, powered with horses, then picked up loose. It was used to feed the livestock.

Planting was done with a horse and hillside plow. A roller was then added to roll the earth down.

For the most part, the early twentieth century farm was completely self-sufficent. The wool from sheep was sold to stores in Marietta. About the only things that were bought were salt, sugar, coffee, and soap. Other products often sold in town were potatoes and various fruits. In addition to these, eggs, milk, and cream were sold on Fridays, usually, in Marietta. The products were taken to town by horse or express (a lighter wagon).

Animals to be butchered were taken first to Elic Smith, who had one of the few sets of scales in the township. After the animals were weighed, they were generally taken to Ed Lanes for butchering.[6]

Tobacco was once a very important cash crop. There were several tobacco packinghouses. Most of these were present in 1800's. The tobacco was packed in big barrels called hogsheads.

For most of the township's history, farming indeed was part of survival. That is not the case today. In fact, very few people in the township today rely on farming as their principal means of support. Instead, farming today for most people serves as a supplement to their livelihoods.

Another very important industry of the past, but lost today was coal. One of the people who talked to us about the coal industry was Jud Strickler, who spent much of his life mining coal

Most of the mining was centered around Moss Run. It began sometime around the 1870's. Jud's father, Carl, and his Uncle Clyde were killed in mine cave-ins. Jud is the grandfather of one of my students, Chris Strickler. Chris, along with another student, Ron Wright, compiled this information about coal mining.

"Entrance to mine on Moss Run"

Much of the coal was used for home fuel. In fact, so many people burned coal on Moss Run that the area became known as "Smoky Hollow." Today, this is County Road 133. Jud estimates there were 25 to 30 mines in this area alone. Another user of coal were all the schools in the township. Some oil wells were drilled with the use of coal. Occasionally, larger contracts were made for coal such as ones with the state to provide coal for building projects. The coal would be used to run machinery.

For the most part, early mines were individually or family owned. However, leases had to be obtained when the mine extended to other's property. The coal was shot off with black rock powder, with fuses set in holes called squibs. Inside the mine, the top was usually five to six feet high. Most of the mines were unsupported inside, and there were as many as 25 rooms in one mine. How far the mine extended depended upon the particular vein. Some mines, according to Jud, extended a mile and a half back. Nearly all the mines were single veins of soft bituminous coal. Usually the coal was screened but in rush seasons, it was sold in chunks. The coal was dug mostly by hand with shovels and picks.

"Smoky Hollow"

In early days, it was taken out by use of small ponies.

it was loaded on wagons and taken out. For the most part,

was sold by the bushel. A good day in the mine would result

:housand bushel production. Carbide lights were used to see

in the mines. In later days, big fans were used for ventilation.

"An old Coal Wagon"

"Gob Pile of Coal"

To say that coal mining was dangerous would indeed be an understatement! With all the sophisticated equipment today, there still are many mine tragedies. Coal mining was but another hard way people of Lawrence made a living.

Most of the coal mining operations ended around 1930. This stemmed mainly from many new state and federal regulations that individuals could not afford to abide by. Secondly, leasing of property became too high and, finally, people by 1930 had alternate ways to heat their homes. Today, there is still a small amount of mining done on Moss Run.[7]

Another important economic aspect of people's lives in the township was the country store. Today, it may seem to be a part of America that has been lost. That is not the case in Lawrence. We still have three such stores. From our research we've tried to gather information on most of the stores that once existed, and there were many scattered all over Lawrence. They were usually the focal point of smaller divisions of the township, such as Bear Run, Sitka, Cow Run, etc. They provided the people with essentials they could not produce for themselves. In addition, they served as a gathering place for discussion of current events, local news, or maybe just a game of checkers. The storekeeper was a friend, and he often extended credit to people to get them through hard times.

The first store in the township was opened by William Powell in 1838, in the upper part of the township, near the corner of Independence Township.[8]

One of the early stores was built by a Mr. Huntsman. His store was located next to the Little Muskingum near where Dean

Eddy's store is today. His store was washed away by the flood of 1898, was rebuilt there and later moved by skids and horses to where Dean's Great-Uncle W. A. Lennington bought the store.

"Dean Eddy's Store"

While Lennington had the store, he became the first postmaster of the newly named community at that time, Dart. John T. Hall purchased the store in 1924 and had it for thirty-three years. For many years John was the backbone of the community. He was especially depended upon during the Great Depression of 1930's. He bought a farm and gave men work. Dean took over the store on October 20, 1958 and runs it today. Dean remodeled the store about three years ago. Prior to becoming owner of the store, Dean had worked in it for John Hall. He is a postmaster today and has moved the post office inside the store. As in the tradition of the store's former owners, Dean can be depended upon to help area residents.[9]

Another place in the township where there was a store for

many years was on Pleasant Ridge. The original one that most people
remember was owned by a Mr. Templeton in 1883. It was success-
ively run and owned by Charles Close, John Sparling, Schramm,
McVey, and John Zimmer, who had it about 1899. Zimmer's was
one of the first local stores to sell clothing such as shirts,
jackets, and pants. Baird Oliver purchased the store from
John Zimmer in 1928, and had it until April 30, 1963, when he
closed it for good.[10]

George Reed had a store in the early 1900's at the mouth of
Moss Run. Bill Lankton had a store at the mouth of Archer's Fork.
Sam Dennis had a store in the early 1900's at Sikta. Dudley
Miller had one of the stores on Cow Run until 1920. One of the
biggest stores was McCauley's, located on Bear Run. Another
store was Heslop's at the foot of Smith Hill. Most of these
stores existed in the early 1900's. Their exact dates of
operations were not obtained.

In addition to Dean Eddy's Store, there are two other
operating general stores in the township. They are Dick Biehl's
and Elmer Miller's.

Biehl's store was originally owned and run by Ike McCowan
in 1860's. Ike's son, Jim, was a doctor at Cow Run for a number
of years before moving to Marietta. The back part of McCowan's
Store was a funeral home with Ike as the undertaker. Pomeroy
McCowan, Ike's other son was the druggist. The back room was
filled with wooden caskets. The store also owned a horse-drawn
hearse. A local joke was that Jim would diagnose the illness,
Pomeroy would prescribe the poison, and Ike would bury the victim.

Dick's father, Delbert Biehl, purchased the store in 1921.
Today, Dick runs the store, thus keeping it in the family for

fifty-five years. Dick says one of the biggest changes in the

"Dick Biehl's Store"

store today is most products are already packaged. It used
to be that most products came in bulk form and had to
be weighed and packaged before selling.[11]

Finally, Elmer Miller's store was opened April 4, 1946.
This was the date of completion. It took approximately nine
months to build the store. Previously, there had been a smaller
store located nearby owned by Glen Hune. Elmer bought this
store and moved it and then added to it at its present location.[12]

(Certainly, there were many more stores and owners than the
ones we have mentioned. This is one of the pitfalls of oral
research. We didn't have the time to talk to everyone who could
have added to this.)

Elmer Miller's Store

Another forgotten industry of past times is the many different mills. At one time there were operating grist, saw, and molasses mills. The old settlement of Lawrence had a grist mill owned by Mr. Hune. In the early 1900's Ed Baltz also owned a grist mill. It was used primarily to grind corn and wheat. There was once a molasses mill located off Route 26, where people could bring their cane. It would be pressed first to extract the juice, then be strained to remove pumies-particles which came through the presser. Finally, it would be boiled down to its finished product. The molasses would be used for sugar and syrup. Many of these such mills were portable. A stationary one was owned by Ed Becker until 1916.[13]

Several saw mills operated in Lawrence. Lawrence Smith bought a sawmill in 1937. He bought timber off people, then cut it and sold it to lumber companies in Marietta. In other sawmills, much chestnut was cut up for making shingles. There was a saw mill on Moss Run for a number of years. Most of these sawmills were powered by steam.

There were several blacksmiths in the township over the years. Walt Henry had a blacksmith shop across from the town hall up until about 1916. Frank Weinstock, who died in 1968, had the most recent one. Frank was the son of an original settler. His shop was located near Biehl's Store. The major job done by blacksmiths was shoeing horses. In addition to this, in earlier days they made wagon wheels as well as many other things.

1. Williams, <u>History of Washington County, Ohio</u>, H. Z.
    Williams and Brothers Publishers, 1881, pp. 663.

2. Ibid, pp. 663-64.

3. Julian Rolston, <u>The First Decade of the Petroleum
    Industry in the Mid-Ohio Valley</u>, pp. 65.

4. Ibid, p. 67.

5. Williams, op. cit., p. 664.

6. Interview with Baird Oliver, March 11, 1976.

7. Interview with Jud Strickler, March 5, 1976.

8. Williams, op. cit., p. 658.

9. Interview with Dean Eddy, March, 1976.

10. Oliver, op. cit.

11. Interview with Dick Biehl, February, 1976.

12. Interview with Elmer Miller, February 23, 1976.

13. Interview with Senior Citizens, March 11, 1976.

"PIONEER DAY"

This chapter was compiled and written by Teresa Becker, Debbie Eddy, Susan Sullivan, Jim Erb, Ken Starkey and Brenda Leister. It's included as part of our book in hopes of preserving many of these lost crafts.

As a contribution to our country's 200th birthday, we, the students of Lawrence Elementary School, planned and succeeded in portraying many of the common chores done in a typical pioneer day. The director and coordinator of "Pioneer Day" was James Mahoney, history teacher at Lawrence.

"Pioneer Day" was held on November 26, 1975. The day consisted of many different activities and age-old arts of the pioneer. Many of the students came dressed in the pioneer fashion. A play about Anne Hutchinson was performed in the morning by the eighth grade class.

Some of the activities were: making apple butter, churning butter, quilting, soap making, and taffy making. Many people from the surrounding area helped in the preparation of "Pioneer Day". Many people also helped in the demonstrations. If it had not been for the many willing and generous people who donated their time to this worthwhile project, our "Pioneer Day" would never have been as successful as it was.

To all those who helped or contributed to this project in any way--Thanks. Your service was greatly appreciated.

"Eighth Graders in Pioneer Dress"

QUILTING

Several members from the senior citizens group demonstrated how to quilt. They were Freda Reed, Nellie Rake, Bernice Farley, Mildred LaFaber and Hilda Fickiesen.

In the pioneer days the pioneers would get together and have a quilting bee. The main reason for this is to have a lot of fun, but still get a lot of work done.

"Ellen Rake & Dorothy DePuy explain
how quilting is done."

KNOTTING COMFORTERS

Jeanie Henthorne, June Gutberlet, Ethel Smith, Shirley
Bowersock and Dorothy DuPuy demonstrated how to knot comforters.
The comforters had the same use as a quilt. They are made on
the same order as a quilt. In the pioneer days the comforters
were not as popular as the quilts.

In order to perform this task you must have a topping (either
pieced or one huge piece of material), a lining (batting) and
the backing.

Both the quilting frames were fairly old. The frames were
hand made of wood. The frames work on a very simple basis. The
quilt or comforter is put on the wheels of the frames. These are
notched in order to move at your rate of knotting or quilting.

"June Gutberlet and Ethel Smith explain
Knotting Comforters"

CROCHETING AND KNITTING

These two crafts have been a part of the pioneer's life
a long time. Afghans, sweaters, and socks were usually knitted
and crocheted for the family. People of all ages could crochet.
It was a craft handed down from generation to generation.

Betty Becker, Juanita Eddy, Karen Burton, and Clara Thompson
brought in some items of their own. They also demonstrated how
to do these age old crafts.

Knitting is a craft in which you use two needles and weave
the yarn between the needles.

FOLK SINGING

A big part of every pioneer's life was folk singing. Many
times families and neighbors would get together for the sole
purpose of singing.

Many of today's popular folk tunes have been handed down
from generation to generation. The main purpose for folk
singing was for entertainment.

As a part of our "Pioneer Day", Mrs. Susan Hontz, music
teacher in the Frontier School District, took each class and sang
a melody of folk songs. These songs ranged in time from the
settling of the west to the Vietnam War.

Folk singing today is just as an important part of American
Heritage as it was 100 years ago.

CANDLE MAKING

Candles were a source of light before the light bulb was
invented. The pioneers would make the candles by the hundreds to
keep up with the demand. The wax was taken from beehives and
melted in a pot. Then a coarse string was dipped into the

wax and hung up to dry. After the string was dry, the process was repeated until the desired width of the candle was reached.

On "Pioneer Day", Cecile Starkey and Karen Goins demonstrated how candles are made. They took wax and melted it, and for coloring they used crayon. To dry the candles, they used cold water.

MUZZLELOADERS

The muzzleloader at one time was a necessity to every pioneer. They needed it for protection and for shooting wild game. The muzzler is somewhat different from a rifle or a shotgun. The main difference between these is the ammunition. In a rifle or shotgun a shell is used, but in a muzzleloader a lead bullet is used. After inserting the bullet, gun powder is then poured. A cap must be put inside the pit beside the firing lock. After this is all done, the muzzleloader is ready to be fired.

On "Pioneer Day" Don Shook and Jerry Eddy displayed and demonstrated the firing of their muzzleloader. Jerry's muzzleloader was one made from a modern day kit. Don Shook's muzzleloader was much older and was passed down to him by past generations.

on Shook fires his muzzleloader."

"Jerry Eddy explains the muzzleloader as James Mahoney fires."

141

SOUR DOUGH MAKING

This process was used in biblical times. Then it was known as leavening. The ingredients consisted of yeast, water, and sugar. This was to germinate the bread. Today it requires 1 cup of starter, add ½ cup of flour, ½ cup of water, 1 teaspoon of sugar and a teaspoon of salt. This is the basis for your sour dough baking. The bread has no kind of shortening.

Ute Kiggans was the demonstrator on the sour dough making. She had several loaves of bread and a coffee cake.

She also had an example of starter and showed us how to store the starter. This process kept the starter from germinating. It is to be refrigerated but not frozen.

INDIAN DISPLAY

The first Americans were Indians. When white men first came to America, they starved because of lack of knowledge of growing food and hunting. The Indians taught the pioneers how to do these things.

The Indians' culture has changed through the years. For example, their hoes, rakes, and cultivators were only pieces of circular-shaped rocks. They would use a long, oval-shaped, very thick rock, preferably granite, for the base of their corn grinder. The actual grinding stone was round. After the corn was ground, they baked it into cornbread.

On "Pioneer Day" , Evelyn Pape and Donna Poynter gave a demonstration on the grinding of corn and how the Indians cultivated their gardens.

Mrs. Pape showed cornbread that she had baked using home ground meal. She also had some arrowheads, pottery, cowhides,

ANTIQUES

On "Pioneer Day" in the old cafeteria there was a display of antiques. There was a corn huller, muzzleloaders brought by Ruth Hunter, an old fashion hand drill, an Edison Standard Phonograph and some other items.

"Mark Binggar demonstrates an old wooden hand drill."

Jan Miller brought in an Edison Standard Phonograph which had several musical cylinders. These cylinders can't be purchased any more.

"Jan Miller with her phonograph"

jewelry and woven baskets.

This was an interesting part of "Pioneer Day" mainly because it presented an almost forgotten part of Indian life.

LYE SOAP MAKING

On "Pioneer Day", Sue Sullivan and Janice Gutberlet demonstrated how to make lye soap. The soap isn't too pleasant smelling, but it is a good cleansing soap.

In order to perform this age old art, women of today use approximately 6 lbs. of melted fat, 1 can of lye and 2½ pts. of hot water. Then you dissolve the lye in the hot water. Let it cool. Then pour the lye solution in a slow easy stream into the melted fat--constantly stirring. Continue stirring until cool. Pour into boxes that have been dipped in cold water. Cut in desired size of squares--when cold, and set.

"Sue Sullivan stirs cooling lye as
Janice Gutberlet stirs hot lye."

TAFFY MAKING

The craft of making taffy is very old. The pioneers used it as a source of entertainment. They would get together and pull the taffy as far as they could.

On "Pioneer Day", Mary Patterson and Cynthia Davis demonstrated The art of making and pulling taffy. They made Salt-Water Taffy.

Ingredients:
1 cup of light corn syrup
2 cups of sugar
1½ cups of water
7 drops of food coloring
¼ teaspoon of flavoring
½ teaspoon of salt
2 teaspoons of butter

Butter the sides and bottom of a 2 quart sauce pan to keep the sugar from sticking. Put the sugar, corn syrup, salt and water in the pan. Cook slowly, stirring constantly till the sugar dissolves. Then cook to hard ball stage or 260° C on a candy thermometer. When dropped into 1 cup of water, it should form a hard ball that is flexible and does not stick to your fingers.

Take the taffy off the heat and add 2 teaspoons of butter, the food coloring, and flavoring--then mix. Then pour on to a buttered surface, till cool.

When cool, pull until it gets stiff, then cut with buttered scissors and wrap in wax paper.

BUTTER CHURNING

In pioneer days there were no fancy stores which stocked butter, but when they did sell butter, it was too expensive for most pioneers to buy. So they made their own from the cream of fresh cows milk.

On "Pioneer Day", Charlotte Lauer and Donna Binegar demonstrated the actual churning of butter.

First you put cream into a churn. Then churn it until it gets real thick. The butter is now starting to form. Add some salt. Then work out the rest of the buttermilk.

"Donna Binegar demonstrates butter
churning."

APPLE BUTTER

Apple butter has been on a pioneer woman's job list for many years. This chore takes a full days work over an open fire. This task often brings tears to the stirrer's eyes, but they are not from hating the chore. They are from the smoke.

On "Pioneer Day", Nancy Eddy, Judy Eddy and Jane Ann Becker made apple butter.

Ingredients:

2½ bushels of apples (Rome Beauty)
15 pounds of sugar
 4 pounds of brown sugar
8-16 3/4 oz. packages of cinnamon drops
 1 bottle-or 4 oz. cinnamon oil

You also need one 13 gallon brass kettle and a wooden paddle.
First make applesauce out of the apples. Then put the applesauce in the kettle for approximately 3 hours, constantly stirring. Then add cinnamon drops. Approximately 2 to 3 hours later add the rest of the ingredients, putting the oil in according to your taste.
Then put the apple butter in jars and seal. When not opened, store jars upside down.

Jane A. Becker stirs apple butter
over an open fire."

"Jane A. Becker stores the apple
butter to be sold."

"Judy Eddy stirs apple butter."

EMBROIDERY

Embroidery is an age old art passed down from mother to daughter since the time of early settlers. Embroidery was used more often for fancy work than for mending.

To embroider you must have a needle. The needle is somewhat like a regular sewing needle, but it has a bigger eye on the end. You need a special kind of thread. To get the design you must iron a transfer on to a light piece of plain colored cloth.

Today women buy kits which contain everything needed to embroider. The kits also have the transfer already ironed on. In pioneer days they had to make their own transfers and had to try hard to obtain the necessary material which was needed.

There are many different stitches in embroidery. Such as: chain stitch, satin stitch, lazy daisy stitch, and outline stitch. Embroidery is individualism.

Milly Spindler, Karen Biehl, and Sandy Matthews demonstrated and displayed some embroidery works of their own on "Pioneer Day".

"Karen Biehl demonstrates
needle point."

Student Comments

"The interviews were always very interesting and fun. We learned something new each time."

Ronald Wright

"...even though a certain area is very small it still can become a very important part of someone's life."

Debbie Morningstar

"...It really made us feel good to write down things about our township."

Christina Becker

"To me this is the greatest experience I have ever had."

Susan Sullivan

"I think in the future it will mean very much to the younger people because someone took time to write a book about their township."

Ken Starkey

"...Some people thought it was a really stupid idea...in the beginning. But after the book was finished they were not that way."

Mark Binegar

"I am awfully glad to have had a part in getting this book together. It has been a great experience for me."

Vesta Minder

"**THE WILDERNESS THAT BECAME LAWRENCE** is a good book and I'm glad I helped even a tiny part."

Ruth Cline

"In writing this book all the kids in our class participated. One of the things I liked best is I know more now about Lawrence Township than before."

Steve Brown

"We feel that student participation is half the fun of working."

Chris Strickler

"I believe that the future classes of our school will find this book useful in studying local history."

Brian Rouse

"We know by far this isn't complete. We just hope it will make an impression of 'we can do it'."

Billy Reed

"A look at the past might help us to understand better how important this project of ours has become. It has gone much further than any of us ever dreamed...

A place full of good people, with kind hearts. A place where people can be proud of who and where they are."

Debra Eddy

In Appreciation

we would like to recognize the individuals who gave of their time to be interviewed:

Dean Becker
Dick Biehl
Dean Eddy
Faye Farley
Bernice Farley
Reed Hanna
June Hendershot
Walter Hoff
Robert Kidd

Mildred LaFaber
Gerald McGregor
Elmer Miller
Baird Oliver
Nellie Rake
Foster Reed
Lawrence Smith
Jud Strickler
Earl Westbrook

www.ingramcontent.com/pod-product-compliance
Lightning Source LLC
Chambersburg PA
CBHW061410090426
42740CB00027B/3496